# Strumming a Rope

# Strumming a Rope

*Huang Fan*

Translators

*Margaret Ross*

*Josh Stenberg*

*Wang Ping*

GP

Gugin Press

New York / Shanghai

ISBN: 979-8-9915011-5-6

Cover: "Yong Zheng Pleasure Picture," Qing Dynasty.
Courtesy of Zheng Lin.

**Gugin Press** is published by
Segue Foundation
300 Bowery FL 2
New York, NY 10012
seguefoundation.com

# Contents

# Preface

Huang Fan's poetry has a breadth of focus that creates many options for translators. This volume, *Strumming a Rope*, with three translators writing from different approaches to translation, allows the reader to see the range of possibilities in the original.

Margaret Ross' accurate and contemporary translations focus readers on the way Huang Fan's logic can be read in her well-turned phrases. Her translations as articulate speech—"I have never seen pigeons argue"—match Huang Fan's earnest treatment of his themes.

Josh Stenberg on the other hand focuses the reader on the fact of translation through his use of lower-case alphabet. Eschewing the formality of case and grammatical punctuation, he instead translates so it's clear how to emphasize each line and stanza. His strategy also emphasizes the equality of words or one might say the subordination of self. Of course, the reader will make their own interpretation of Stenberg's lowercase usage.

Wang Ping, as a native speaker and an English professor, captures a full range of Huang Fan's poetry by reminding us of the English language's ability to truncate poetry lines by eliminating articles and particles and focusing on the poet's nouns—"Opening the clam with hands." With Poundian juxtaposition and contemporary humor, she materializes the English to keep us reading for greater clarity.

Not being a Chinese speaker, I enjoyed editing these translations for their differences and their ability to capture different aspects of Huang Fan's writing. Sometimes *poète maudit*, sometimes modernist absurdist, sometimes as he himself says "a saint using humor and ridicule," Huang Fan takes full advantage of metaphor's ability to scale in all directions and bring our worlds together. The similarities and differences between the poet's identity in China and the US always make it worthwhile having the chance to choose from multiple views.

*James Sherry*
*New York*

# Huang Fan

Margaret Ross Translations

## 海边的除夕

落日的骨头，在大海沸腾的水里炖着
谁也不知，这锅汤是为谁准备的

我的房间，刚好朝向海
一整夜可以看见，烟花在空中划出的祈祷

海边的灯塔，没有机会冥想
它在船失明时，要抛给船员光的缆绳

我在沙滩留下一串脚印，像感谢着什么
是啊，倘若春天来了，我们就可以省下抑郁

## NEW YEAR'S BY THE SEA

The boiling sea stews the bones of the sunset
No one knows who this soup is for

My room faces the water
All night, I see fireworks draw prayers in the sky

A lighthouse by the sea has no chance to meditate
When boats go blind, it's got to toss them bright ropes

I left footprints in the sand like I was grateful for something
Right—if it's spring, we can save on depression

## 陀螺

它不屑于四平八稳
也永远不会跪下
哪怕最终会倒下，也要挺直脊梁

它一鞭一鞭，承受着抽打
旋转着苦难的华尔兹
它只能幻想自己是太阳
把飞来的鞭子，看作是绕它打转的行星

它的脚尖，已磨得嘶嘶作响
它把脚尖当钻头，对准大地
就算花费一生，仍无法在大地扎根

它没有眼睛
却靠把自己转晕的苦役，为飞机找到航向
当它累得最终倒下，那个叫风的伴侣
竟立刻弃它而去

## SPINNING TOP

It disdains caution
Never kneels
Even though it's going to fall
It holds its spine straight

Lash by lash, it withstands its whipping
Spins in its suffering waltz
It can only imagine itself as a sun
Orbited by a whip

Its toe hisses
Its toe is a drill aimed at Earth
All its life it's been drilling but it can't take root

It has no eyes
Relies on the dizzying work of spinning for a flight path
When it's so tired it topples over, its friend the wind
Abandons it

## 杯子

杯子，是张开的嘴
你每天与它亲吻
你喝下的白开水，是河水清澈的心

杯子，也是一只瞪圆的眼
杯里的茶水，是棕色瞳仁
它每天瞪着会说假话的你

你喝水时，听懂了杯子的倾诉声么?
你是否看见，寂静最喜欢住在杯中?
你吹动茶水时的涟漪
是杯子收藏的文字，你信不信?

杯子从小失去了双腿
它把你的手当翅膀，在屋里飞翔
你喝完，不管给它留下什么
它都把你的唇印，当作你与它结婚的公章

深夜，黑暗也会装满它
让已经离去的你，成为它百般思念的黎明

## CUP

A cup is an open mouth
You kiss each day
The water you drink is the river's clear heart

A cup is an eye
Its brown pupil of tea
Glares every day at you, liar

Do you hear a cup's voice when you drink water?
See how a cup is the chosen nest of silence?
When you blow on tea, your cup
Saves every word the ripples write—do you
 believe that?

Since childhood, this cup has been legless
Your hands are wings to fly it through the room
Even if you drain it, leaving it nothing
It thinks your lip print is a marriage contract

At night, the cup brims with darkness
You are the dawn it longs for

## 鸽子

从没见鸽子争吵过
只看见它们静静地飞翔
从不知，鸽子是否分天真或世故?
只知，它们没有让自己劳累一生的往事

也许它们就是空气的舌头
懒得说轿车装满的叹息
也许它们在屋脊排着队
争着当白雪结婚的司仪

直到有一天，我从窗口抬头
发现飞翔就是它们的祖国——
飞翔，让我的沉默失去了内容
谢天谢地——是它们
教会了我如何谈论祖国

当我站在鸽群下，突然觉得
人啊，甚至都比不上一朵
向鸽子仰头致意的鲜花

PIGEONS

I've never seen pigeons argue
I only see them soar
I don't know if a pigeon is naïve or worldly
I just know it has no past to make it toil through life

Maybe they're the tongues of the air
Lazily expressing cars' sighs
Maybe they're lined up on the roof
Vying to perform snow's wedding

One day I stick my head out the window
And realize their nation is the act of soaring
Soaring makes my silence meaningless
Thank god, they've taught me how to talk
   about nations!

Standing under a flock of pigeons, I think *oh*
*People aren't even worth one flower blooming*
   *toward them*

# 盐

一颗颗盐，就是一滴滴结冰的泪
帮我数着历史上的灾难
我不能怪罪，它望着美食说：
这里面都是伤口

它怀念曾在大海里的自由
现在，它带着对波涛的记忆跃入汤中
却只找到脸的倒影
隐身成为牙齿无法对付的软

某天深夜，它跟随一股冷汗
令我从噩梦中惊醒
梦里的血含着盐的咸味
犹如人的挫折中，有神的沉默

游过了大海，汤水对它
就只是浅浅的水塘
吃饭对它，竟变成残酷的收监

某天，它用很重的咸味令我拼命咳嗽
我的喉咙仿佛摸到了冰冷的鱼刺
也许，它只是告诉我：
我就要去你的身体里坐牢
你总不该忘记，我究竟是谁吧？

## SALT

Grain by grain, salt's frozen tears
Help me count history's disasters
I can't blame salt for telling food
*You're full of wounds*

Salt misses the freedom of the ocean
Remembering waves, salt jumps into a soup
But it finds there only my reflected face
It hides by making itself too soft to chew

Sometimes, salt follows a cold sweat
Waking me from a nightmare
Dreamed blood tastes like salt
As if in human failure lay the silence of God

Having swum in the ocean
Salt considers soup a shallow pond
For salt, every meal is a jail

One day, an extra salty flavor
Makes me cough and cough
It feels like cold fish bones scraping my throat
Maybe it's salt telling me
*I'm going to prison in your body*
*Don't ever forget who I am!*

## 红葡萄

为了看清这世界的险恶
还在枝头，它已瞪红了眼
直到信任夏风吟唱的赞歌
为了成为血的波涛，它把一生都献给了酒窖

我的杯里，是它青春的血
试着在我心里掀起波涛
它也成了跨上我血流的骑手
一下就松开了我年龄的缰绳——

我说了平时不说的脏话
差点吓醒墓里的亲人
那一夜，我抱着爱情呼呼大睡
醒来却找不到爱人

我混迹于城市的盛宴
终于明白，爱情是红酒的税收
它用密集的税，让红酒变得高贵

一车皮的红葡萄酒
就是一车皮的凡高，你信不信?
一车皮的红葡萄
就是一车皮的乳头，你信不信?

## RED GRAPES

In order to see the world's evils clearly
They redden their eyes on the vine
Until they believe the warm wind's praise
In order to become waves in our blood
They offer their lives to the wine cellar

In my glass, the blood of their youth
Tries to send waves through my heart
It's a jockey riding my bloodstream
Loosening age's reins—

I used dirty words I don't normally use
Nearly scaring awake my dead relatives
I fell fast asleep with my arms around love
But, waking, couldn't find my lover

I fit right in at dinner in the city
And finally realize love is wine's tax
High taxes make wine noble

A crate of red wine
Is a crate of Van Goghs—do you believe that?
A crate of red grapes
Is a crate of nipples—do you believe that?

## 地铁

每个人的心底，都有一列地铁
准时把你载到人群的深渊
让你天天，与某个大师擦肩而过

你总把自己想象成人群中的钉子
渴望扎疼一个富人
如同扎疼一个你不常用的词
某个姑娘红脸的一瞬
其实也替一首诗找到了比喻

拥挤的地铁，无法为你的彬彬有礼
腾出不受打扰的空隙
你在拥挤中变成了另一个人——
用酋长对抗处长
用流感对抗爱情
用恍惚对抗流言

你喜欢在人群中毫不起眼
这让你的叹息也充满羡慕
你甚至羡慕，地铁有一只仁慈的胃——
它每天吃下你、排出你
却让你毫发无损

对地铁，我说不上爱或恨
它更像一只药瓶
每天装进我这颗胶囊
让我准时到达那只教室的胃——
为一群学生，治愈他们的背叛

## SUBWAY

Through the bottom of everyone's heart runs a subway
Delivering you to the crowd's abyss
Making you every day brush up against some genius

You imagine yourself as a nail in the crowd
Longing to pierce a rich man
Like a word you rarely use
A girl's sudden blush
Is a poem finding its metaphor

A packed subway can't be polite to you
So it forms a protected space
In the crowd, you become another person—
Pitting a chief against a chair
Pitting the flu against love
Stupor against gossip

You like not being noticed in the crowd
You're free to sigh with envy
You even envy the subway's merciful stomach—
Every day it eats you, excretes you
And leaves you unscathed

I can't say I love or hate the subway
It's more like a pill bottle
Loaded with this pill I am
Each day, it sends me to the belly of the classroom
To cure student traitors

## 礼貌

礼貌，能让一个坏人貌似友好
能让一个仇人张开虚伪的双臂
能让一个异乡人，以为在家乡
甚至以为一阵凄厉的北风，也会带来爱情

日子不断流动，礼貌
却在查找任性的陌生人
要把一匹野马，变成一个羞答的新娘
有时，礼貌真是一副锁链
一寸一寸锁住我们的脏话

如果没有脏话，谁能把学生从老师的手里救出?
谁能把人民从政治的手里救出?
谁能把眼睛从悲伤的泪水中救出?
谁能把耳朵从城市的喧闹中救出?
甚至在爱情的最深处，一对颤抖的乳房
也需要脏话细心呵护

可是，礼貌在我的国度还没有恢复
一个人的彬彬有礼，会被视为懦弱
没有礼貌的国度，就像砍光树木的大山
温暖无处可藏，也是一个刑场

我像大雪一样低下头来
思考铁一样生锈的礼貌
如果我额头发烧，一定与礼貌有关
如果有人想自杀，一定与礼貌有关

## GOOD MANNERS

Manners can make a bad guy look friendly
Make your enemy open fake arms
Make a foreigner think he's home
Think even a sharp north wind brings love

Days flow, but manners
Seek capricious strangers
They want to turn a wild horse into a shy bride
Sometimes manners are actually chains
Tightening around curse words

Without curse words, who could rescue students
  from teachers?
People from politics?
Eyes from tears?
Ears from the noise of the city?
Even in the depths of love, a pair of trembling breasts
Need curse words to take care of them

But manners haven't returned to my country
If you act polite here, you're seen as weak
Mannerless countries are deforested mountains
There's nowhere to stow warmth. It's a death chamber

I am like snow lowering its head
Thinking about rusty manners
If my forehead feels hot, that's related to manners
If someone wants to kill himself, that's related to manners

## 汤勺

我们和汤勺成不了朋友
哪怕喝汤时，我们深情地看着它
我们衣锦荣华，它却总把自己倒空
它要倒掉让地球变穷的山珍与海味

它宁愿空着眼窝，也不要汤水给它眼睛
它拒绝阅读坟场一样的菜单
有时，我似乎听见它谈起久别未归的故乡——
那锈黑了河水的矿山，曾经是啄木鸟弹琴的琴房

我们买再多的汤勺，也和汤勺成不了朋友
它宁愿空着眼窝，也不想和我们交换眼神
宁愿不穿衣裳，也不拔一根草取暖
只愿用清脆的嗓音，和瓷碗谈心

我不记得，已买过多少汤勺
我努力学习，这空眼窝的盲诗人的语言
看戏之前，试着用喝汤的声音，道出它内心的巨响

## SPOONS

We can never befriend spoons
We gaze at them tenderly, slurping soup
We dress in bright clothes, but they strip themselves
Pouring away delicacies plundered from the earth

A spoon prefers its socket empty, doesn't want soup
  to give it an eye
Doesn't want to read the menu's epitaphs
Sometimes, I think I hear a spoon describe its
  long-lost village—
The river blackened by a mine that used to echo
  with woodpeckers

No matter how many spoons we buy, we can't befriend them
A spoon prefers its socket empty, doesn't want to meet
  our eyes
It wants to stay naked, won't wear a single blade of grass
It only uses its silvery voice to confide in the bowl

I don't remember how many spoons I've bought
I study the language of this blind poet's sockets
I eat soup before I go to the theater
And try to slurp the roar of the spoon's interior

## 汉与英

——在冬日的弗蒙特，与美国友人谈语言

我的汉语，是你英语的密码
你丢了密码本
我说的粗话，已不会让你脸红

你的英语，是我汉语的密码
你说得再多，你的话也像这里的雪
让我问路的脚印，全都走错

我带来的汉语是一支歌
歌词像脚印，纷纷掉在地上
它们说，我们是冬天的标签
却不知该贴到哪种酒瓶上?

要听懂铁锹的劳动，还需要语言吗?
我合上英语课本，突然明白
没有皱纹的雪，最能称出劳动的重量

这里的大雪，说着另一种语言
它把造出的新词，撒满天空
填充着汉语和英语的空洞

## CHINESE AND ENGLISH

*discussing language with a friend*
*on a winter day in Vermont*

My Chinese is your coded English
For which you've lost the key
If I talk dirty, you won't blush

Your English is my coded Chinese
No matter how much you say, your speech is like the snow
Leading my feet astray

The Chinese I brought here is a song
Footprints are its lyrics
They say *we're winter's labels*
*Which liquor bottles should we stick to?*

Do you really need language to understand
The sound of a shovel digging?
I close the English book and realize
Work is best weighed on untouched snow

The snow here speaks another language
It sows new words across a sky
Filling gaps in Chinese, in English

## 被子

被子是蟒蛇，白天盘在床头
晚上把你吞入腹中
梦是它的胃，你每晚都成功逃出
清晨，当你下床，它饿得只剩一张皮

被子是情人，当你弃它而去
它气得病入膏肓，把自己蜷得像一座坟墓
当你晚上哄它，它又把你揽入怀中
鼾声是你的情话，哄得它呼呼大睡

被子是蜂巢，你是蜜蜂
当你满载而归
你向它吐出最甜蜜的梦
时常，梦的甜蜜又被诗人偷吃

被子是闲话，一辈子都裹着你
黑夜漫长，你在与闲话的搏斗中
等待着天明

## BLANKET

A blanket is a python, coiled at the foot of the bed by day
Swallowing you by night
Dreams are the stomach you manage each night to escape
When you rise in the morning, the python's so hungry
It's nothing but skin

A blanket is a lover, sick with rage when you leave
It hunches up like a tombstone
But when you coax it at night, it hugs you back
Snores are your sweet talk, lulling it to sleep

A blanket is a hive and you're a bee
Back from gathering pollen
You spit out sweet dreams
Dreams poets like to eat in secret...

A blanket is gossip, following you all your life
All night you wrestle against it
Waiting for daylight

## 南京夜曲

九点
月亮开始长出乌亮的长发
让男人着迷，如同灯
让蛾子着迷

十点
我们——黑夜的仆人
一同戴上它的墨镜

十一点
脚步声闯进了梦里
成为阴险的敲门声

零点
没有谁比醒着的人更孤独
安眠药，只是不让焦虑爆炸

一点
树根翘起腿来
绊倒了一个夜行者

两点
一个，两个，醉鬼
被月亮的银斧
劈倒

三点
灯下站岗的影子，多么想
被飞翔的梦蒸发

四点
在梦里爬行的爱情
用露珠舔着伤口

## NANJING NIGHT SONG

9:00
The moon grows bright black hair
and lures men like light
lures moths

10:00
Us: night's servants
putting on our sunglasses

11:00
The sound of footsteps enters a dream
and turns into sinister knocking

12:00
No one's lonelier than someone awake now—
all sleeping pills do is keep anxiety from exploding

1:00
A tree root kicked
and tripped a night walker

2:00
One drunk, two drunks
split by the silver axe
of the moon

3:00
A shadow on duty under the lamp
longs for a flying dream to evaporate it

4:00
Love crawls through a dream
licking wounds with dew

五点
银河开始碎成锁链
锁住了晨读的学子

六点
旭日不知羞耻
开始颁发它的委任状

5:00
The Milky Way breaks down into chains
to lock up students reading at dawn

6:00
A shameless sunrise
starts to appoint its proxies

## 帽子

风一来，头上的帽子就想跳崖
想倒光它装满的黑暗
想抱住地上青草的卑微命运
它不喜欢被我顶礼，高高在上

它要像柳条那样，弯下腰去
看虫蚁花草没有一个穿着衣裳
地上的纸屑、痰迹，也拥有自己的忧伤
它不知道，它用口含住的这颗头颅
其实是一滴浑浊的大泪珠

我坐在山间的风口
知道它像一只鸟，想回到正在盘旋的鸟群
知道它对我，早已日久生厌

当风把它吹落在地
心高气傲的我，也只得向它弯腰低头——
拾起帽子的一瞬
我认出，它就是儿时的我啊

## HAT

When the wind blows, my hat wants to leap off my head
Wants to pour away the shadows inside it
To embrace the lowly fate of grass
It doesn't like how I honor it, raising it high

It wants to be a willow branch, bending down
Seeing how naked the flowers and bugs are
How litter and spit have their sorrows too
How could my hat know the head in its mouth
Is really a big muddy tear?

I sit at a windy spot in the mountains
Knowing my hat is a bird longing to rejoin the flock
Knowing I've bored my hat for years

When the wind blows my hat to the ground
Proud me is forced to bow my head—
When I pick up my hat, it occurs to me
My hat is my childhood self

## 茶叶

茶叶泡在水里，就成为水的柳眉
成为水的细腰、长腿和手指
它不出声，像哑剧演员
模仿我慵懒的睡姿

茶叶泡在水里，就成为春天的潜水艇
雾霾再也征服不了它
我隔着玻璃杯，打量这隐士的幸福
想着，它从前是否有过烦恼？

水，也是盖在它头上的透明婚纱
帮它完成与我的动人婚礼
有时，水也大哭一场
仿佛对我说：你看它瘦骨嶙峋
却把仅剩的温暖都献给你

我一次次倒入开水
直到茶叶再也泡不出茶味——
它用失神的目光，仿佛对我说：
我已到暮年，身体发胖变丑
亲爱的，别犹豫
你该去迎娶苗条的新茶了

## TEA LEAVES

As they steep, they become the water's eyebrows
Become its slim waist, its thighs and fingers
They're mute as mimes
Mimicking my sleeping body

As they steep, they become spring's submarine
Never again will smog defeat them
Here on the other side of the cup, I size up these hermits
I wonder—do they worry? Fear?

Hot water is tea's wedding veil
To crown tea's marriage to me
Sometimes the water cries
As if to say *look how skinny the bride is*
*And still she offers you her last scrap of warmth*

I pour and repour boiling water
Until all flavor's seeped from the tea leaves
Their glum look says
*I'm old—my body's swollen—*
*Darling, don't hesitate*
*Go marry some skinny new tea*

## 老婆

我可以谈论别人，却无法谈论老婆
她的优点和缺点，就如同我的左眼和右眼——
我闭上哪一只，都无法看清世界

她的青春，已从脸上撤入我的梦中
她高跟鞋的叩响，已停在她骨折的石膏里
她依旧有一副玉嗓子
但时常盘旋成，孩子作业上空的雷霆

我们的烦恼，时常也像情爱一样绵长
你见过，树上两片靠不拢的叶子
彼此摇头致意吗?只要一方出门
那两片叶子就是我们

有时，她也动用恨
就像在厨房里动用盐——
一撮盐，能让清汤寡水变成美味
被盐腌过的食物，才能放得更长久

我可以谈论别人，却无法谈论老婆
就像牙齿无法谈论舌头
一不小心，舌头就被牙齿的恨伤害
但舌头的恨，像爱一样，永远温柔

## MY WIFE

I can talk about other people, but I can't discuss my wife
Her merits and faults are my left and right eyes
If I try to shut either, I can't see clearly

Having left her face, her youth lives in my dreams
A cast on her leg hushed her high-heeled clicking
She still has a jade throat
But it often yells at the kids' unfinished homework

Our worries seem as enduring as love
Have you ever seen leaves at either end of a branch
Nodding toward each other? Whenever one of us goes out
She and I are those leaves

Sometimes she uses hate
Like salt in cooking
A pinch of salt turns a meager meal into a delicacy
Only food cured in salt can keep

I can talk about other people, but I can't discuss my wife
Just as teeth can't discuss the tongue—
If they aren't careful, their hate injures the tongue
But the tongue's hate is just like love, always tender

## 蚊子

翻开书，一只蚊子突然飞来
它用嗡嗡嗡的哭声，倾述我是它的初恋?
它要用针一样的舌头
把绵绵情话注入我的血流?

我皮肤上的红包痒着
它到底把什么，埋入了这红色的坟丘?
我皮肤上的红土堆啊，越来越多
它继续挖呀掘呀，是为了掩埋它死去的孩子?

有一刻，我与它相互对望
它肚子鼓胀，分明是一个孕妇
为了子孙，它放弃了苗条的身材
它用嗡嗡嗡的哭声，仿佛说:
我今夜就要产卵，请放过我!

我放下一直跟踪它的手
开始像体贴情人那样，忍受被它咬伤的疼痛

## MOSQUITO

When I open my book, a mosquito appears
Does it cry *wung wung wung* to tell me I'm its first love?
Does it want to use its needle tongue
To inject me with sweet talk?

On my skin, red envelopes itch
What's buried in those red graves?
Mounds multiply on my skin
Is that mosquito digging and digging
To bury a dead child?

For a moment, we look at each other
With its bulging belly, it's clearly a pregnant woman
Giving up her figure for a child
She cries *wung wung wung* as if to say
*I'm about to give birth! Please let me go*

I put down the hand that's been tracking her
And start to act like a doting lover, enduring bites

## 玉

你的肩上背着皇帝
你一放下，一个朝代就崩塌了

你的耳里，满是太监的尖叫
你想远行的双脚，长在宫女迈不出宫的腿上

你是皇帝掌心的月亮
照亮过宫廷的每个阴谋

你是没有骨头的骨头
没有色彩的色彩

没有人知道，你肌肤如丝
舌头却冰如刺刀

## JADE

You carry a king on your shoulders
As soon as you lower him, the dynasty topples

The eunuch's screams ring in your ear
Your feet ache to travel but belong to the legs of
  a palace maid

You're the moon in the emperor's palm
Illuminating every plot in court

You're a boneless bone
A colorless color

Your skin is silk, so nobody knows
Your tongue's an icy dagger

## 高压

我想象，自己就生活在海洋深处
无法像向日葵，每天向升起的太阳致敬
无论在水中种什么，都不会有收获
甚至不知，是哪些海水的白牙，在和我作对?

海中那突然的冷潮，想把我留在水的刑具里
深海的漆黑，就像瓶中的墨水
自己没有力气爬到纸上，去挑选真理

哪怕我再狂，像魟一样成为水中的浮云
海也是污染过的，到处隐忍着美丽的毒斑
哪怕我竭力搓洗，身上还是粘满是非的寄生虫

也许我只能像鱼卵那样，和上升的水泡一起高歌:
跟着海潮，我并没有原地踏步!

## HIGH PRESSURE

I think I live deep in the ocean
Powerless to be a sunflower daily facing dawn
Whatever I plant down here comes to nothing
Are the water's white teeth bared against me?

The quick cold currents want to leave me to their torment
The darkness is like darkness lodged in an ink bottle
Without the strength to climb onto paper, to leap
    into the truth

Even if I were wild as a stingray, a floating cloud
    in the water
The ocean would be polluted, full of gorgeous poisons
I scrub my body as hard as I can, but it's infested with
    right and wrong
Maybe all I can do is sing along with the roe
Singing along with the water bubbles
If I go with the tide, I must be making progress!

## 旧邮筒

一只旧邮筒，无人使用
住在雨的帐篷里。从早到晚
它大口吞进有毒的雾霾
吐出更宽大的虚无

它的影子在身边转来转去
仿佛儿子向父亲忏悔

它老了，但从不戴眼镜
大风也吹不倒它
唯有它懂得，沉默有谁也颠覆不了的重心

它看出，志得意满的闪电
不过是天际的裂纹
听出，隆隆雷鸣
不过是上帝迷路的叫喊

面对一条条马路发出的邀请，它只张开嘴——
既不答应也不回避
既无粗话，也不歌唱

## THE OLD MAILBOX

The old mailbox no one uses
Lives under the rain's tent. All day
It swallows pollution
Exhales an even richer nothingness

Its shadow orbits it
Like a repentant son

It's old but it doesn't wear glasses
And wind can't knock it down
It knows silence has a center
Of gravity no one can topple

It sees proud lightning
Is a crack in the horizon
It understands thunder
Is a lost god shouting

At the streets' invitations, it opens its mouth—
Since it doesn't accept and doesn't refuse them
It's neither cursing nor singing

## 停电

那时，全城会让出灯光
让它照料郊外忙碌的抽水机
照亮在夜间抢收的农民
只剩我一人，诅咒这照不亮唐诗的黑暗

黑暗中，家人都成了陌生人
表情丰富的脸，骤然一贫如洗
我们只剩下院子上方那只月亮的眼睛
读着夜空不朽的贫穷

偶尔，奶奶也会让烛光展开短翅
让它用暗淡的丝绸，盖住我的睡眠
奶奶像深夜的哨兵，继续用纳鞋的针
在我的梦里留下巡逻的脚印

如今，白天早已壮大到了深夜
黑暗竟像苗条的女子
连她也要侧着身子
才能穿过城市灯火的空隙

已在我眼里扎根的灯火啊
正是这枚没有尽头的金币
令我开始怀念四十年前停电的那些深渊

## BLACKOUTS

Back then, the whole city went without light
So light could shine on the rural water pumps
Could shine on farmers harvesting through the night
Only I cursed the dark
I couldn't read my Tang poems

The dark turned family into strangers
Each intricate face became something destitute
We had only the moon's eye over the courtyard
Reading the night sky's poverty

Sometimes Grandma let a candle spread its short wings
And draw dull silk across my sleep
Grandma was a watchman using her awl
To patrol my dreams

In the city now, day extends through the night
And darkness is a slim woman
Turning sideways
To slip through the narrow gaps in light

The light that's taken root in my eyes
Is a gold coin so wide, it never ends
It makes me miss those blackouts forty years ago

## 白口罩

—2020年春天札记

它像一只素手，突然捂住我的脸
已两个月，我仍不适应
它捂暖我叹息的拥抱
我说出的母语，也应该被它好好过滤？

它是舌头的牢门，关住了多少大言不惭
它让爱情，也不要靠得太近
它说我们的嘴像伤口，需要它来紧紧包扎
它像白月亮那样，让我在梦中埋下一点奢望

它是今春开得最盛的白花
试图与悲伤的颜色相称
它也是病人肺里的冬天
想在众人的脸上长久结冰
让我抱怨时，像含着满口的愧疚

# WHITE FACE MASK

*notes on spring 2020*

It's like a white hand pressed over my face
After two months, I'm still not used to
Its embrace warming my sighs
Should it filter my language too?

It's a prison door for the tongue. It shuts up the boasting
It won't let love get too close
It says our mouths are wounds and must be bandaged
It's like the moon, letting me bury a little wild hope
    in a dream

It's the most common flower blooming this spring
Trying to match the color of grief
It's also the winter inside sick lungs
It wants to freeze every face for a long time
When I complain, my mouth fills with guilt

## 失去的，都会回来

失去的，都会回来
回到别人的命运，回到谈心展开的幸福
回到陌生人的致意

连掉落的黑发，也回到漆黑的文字
回到书中的山洪
牵动我发根的思想

我的初恋，也回到一个男孩
更高亢的誓言，刚刚平伏一个女孩的叫骂
他俩掠过大街的爱情
让我像当年一样提心吊胆

我那跳楼自杀的同学，他的生命
也回到郊外落日的孤寂，回到傍晚的鸟鸣——
而城里的喧哗，依旧没有一缕忧思

我故去的父亲，雨水正湿润他的墓
树木已吸足他的想法，挺直了他的腰杆
检阅着风说的话:“是该知道的时候了!”

没有谁，再能从我这儿夺走什么
就连广场上抹去的脚印，也回到钟山、郊外
用它无用的漫游，勾勒出一个秋天的自由

当然，我已遗忘得太多，但也只是仿佛遗忘
它们都已回到梦中，醒来
继续用空气的指甲，检查我的舌头——

## EVERYTHING LOST WILL RETURN

Everything lost will return
Return as someone else's destiny, return
In the pleasure of recounting it
Return in a stranger's greeting

Even lost hairs return as black script
Return as the mountain stream in a book
Nudging thoughts from my hair roots

My first love returns as a boy
Shouting promises at a girl
Who's only just stopped yelling at him
Flitting about on the street, their love
Returns me to my old anxieties

And my friend who jumped off a roof to kill himself, his life
Returns in the silence of suburban sunsets, in evening
    birdsong—
But the city noise stays carefree

Rain moistens my father's grave
The trees inhale his thoughts, straighten his posture
They inspect the wind's words: it's time you knew!

No one can take a thing away from me
Even those footprints erased from the Square
Return to the mountain, the countryside
They use their useless wandering to trace an autumn freedom

Of course, I've forgotten too much
But all of it only seems forgotten
It's returned in dreams. When I wake
Air's finger examines my tongue—

舌头没有沉默啊
它是要找一副降落伞，再往深渊里跳——
谁的一生，不是一副跳向深渊的降落伞？

The tongue isn’t reticent
It wants a parachute to jump into the void
And whose life isn’t a parachute?

# Huang Fan

Josh Stenberg Translations

## 中年

青春是被仇恨啃过的，布满牙印的骨头
是向荒唐退去的，一团热烈的蒸汽
现在，我的面容多么和善
走过的城市，也可以在心里统统夷平了

从遥远的海港，到近处的钟山
日子都是一样陈旧
我拥抱的幸福，也陈旧得像一位烈妇
我一直被她揪着走……
更多青春的种子也变得多余了
即便有一条大河在我的身体里
它也一声不响。年轻时喜欢说月亮是一把镰刀
但现在，它是好脾气的宝石
面对任何人的询问，它只闪闪发光……

## middle age

youth: hatred-gnawed, bones scored with toothmarks
recedes into the absurd, a knot of ardent steam
now my features are so genial
the cities i've passed through can all be razed in the heart

from the faraway harbor to bell mountain near at hand
all days are equally stale
the contentment in my arms is stale as a chaste widow
she's always tugging at me to go....
and any further seeds of youth have become superfluous
even if a great river rushes through my body
it is soundless. as a young man, i liked to say the moon
    was a sickle
but now it is a sweet-tempered gemstone
and faced with any query, all it ever does is shimmer...

## 城市之歌

熟悉的服饰，熟悉的车流
熟悉的街巷中的落日
熟悉的街头的斗殴，只一瞬
我就厌恶了眼前的一切

是一场刚结束的阵雨，打开了清新
是鲁莽闯入的坏消息，在防止中年的钙流失
是的，生活不能只用新的街道来验收——
仰望高楼，我惊恐于什么都以祖国的名义……

我们的城市无边广大，但有什么值得我们去热爱？
活下去，成了唯一的江山
平庸，成了我们周身的血
我们的口号绰绰有余，我们的亲人寥寥无几

## song of the city

familiar clothing, familiar traffic flow
familiar sunsets in the streets, alleys
familiar street brawls, and in the blink of an eye
i was filled with loathing for everything in sight

it was just after a rain shower, freshness opening
bad news barging rudely in, halting that midlife calcium loss
indeed, life cannot be verified or accepted only in terms
of new roads—
i look up at the skyscrapers and panic to see everything
named after the fatherland…

our city is vast beyond measure, but what has it got
worth loving?
survival has become the only land
banality has converted our whole body's blood
we have too many slogans, too few loved ones

# 郊游

枫叶灼人，它们像灯光
照着一个人的失眠
再大的心愿，这时也更单薄
更虚弱了……

摸一摸枫叶，想一想它们的心
是多么徒劳啊……
一只灰鸠飞过，更增添了枫林的神秘

就这样踱步、失语，到处是心悦诚服啊
人就像这条山溪，已经干涸了
还要从木桥下迂回穿过……

## excursion

maple leaves sear us like lanterns
shining upon some insomniac
hope may be ever so large but now grows flimsier
feebler…

feel these maple leaves, remember how their hearts
are so much in vain…
a grey turtledove flies overhead adding to the
   maple grove's mystery

to just wander like this, speechless, everywhere such
   cheerful admiration
a human is like this mountain brook, dry
and yet it winds its way beneath the wooden bridge,
   and onwards…

## 快递至南京的鲜花

友人快递给我的鲜花
被家人遗忘在快递房
没人知道它心里的绝望
十五天没人搭理它——

每个来取包裹的人
它都以为，是来找它的家人
直到对方离去的背影，让它感到寒凉

后来它打算爱上快递房
在收了租费的屋里
设法体会免费居住的幸福

当它枯成一个老太婆
它仅剩的孤独，也被快递员
扔进垃圾车，化为下落不明的尘埃

听完它的故事，我才发现
我已辜负了多少造物的一生啊

## fresh flower sent by courier to nanjing

a friend couriered me a fresh flower
my family forgot it in the depot
no one knew the flower's despair
forgotten fifteen days

each time someone came for a package
the flower thought one of us had come for it
until that someone turned and left: blooms shiver

later it resolved to love the depot
that rented space
settled for the contentment of living rent free

withered to an old crone
what remained was solitude, the courier
threw it in the trash truck, to disintegrate
who knows where

only when i'd heard the whole tale did i realize
how many living things i've let down, their whole life long

## 门环

烧红的铁，在锻打中尖叫
令铁匠身旁的树，也在哀痛
风不能再像往日那样，只顾向我问候
它也教我的衣裳，试着张嘴叫喊

每一记的锻打，是为了完成谁的惩罚？
或者铁匠从灼热的铁中，瞥见了铁的野性
他要用锻打，使之驯服
使之成为木门上的圆满门环

当我摸着院门的门环
我会想，它身躯里的野性仍在发酵吗？
那一记记的锻打，它曾用什么来消化？
我摸着它生锈的身躯，仿佛想摸出
那曾崭新的青春，是否还在它的心里？

小时我喜欢看炉火中烧红的铁
想象自己是铁匠，让它听我摆布
如今，我摸着门环弯曲的脊梁
分明摸出了藏在我心中的野性

## the knocker

red-hot iron is shrieking in the forge
the trees near the blacksmith groan in sympathy
the wind can no longer simply greet me as before
it too teaches my clothing to open its mouth and shout

when something is forged, whose punishment
    is accomplished?
or has the blacksmith glimpsed iron's savagery in the
    molten mass
so that forging is a discipline
to form it into round knocker for wooden door

when i touch the knocker on the courtyard door
i always think, is the savagery in its body still fermenting?
how has it digested each forging?
i touch its rusted body like i'm touching forth
that brand-new springtime—is it still there in its heart?

as a kid i used to enjoy watching the red-hot iron
    in the flames
imagined myself as a blacksmith, the iron submitting
    to my will
but now, when i touch the knocker's curved spine
it's clear that what i touch is my own heart's savagery

## 龙

龙原来是什么，已不重要
只要它可以让节日，在春天发芽
只要有人扮演它时，一些人的心里有收获
只要地上的雪水，也想穿上过节的新鞋
只要吱呀打开的家门，像久别重逢的眼睛
把来客深情端详

风送来了节日的气味
龙在街上，被鞭炮贴上烟雾的邮票——
人要把平安的祷告，寄往来年

原本是兽的眼睛，似从烟雾中露出一丝困惑——
人已习惯用爆炸，制造喜悦？
奔波一年才过完的生活
要用雷声来总结？

我小时爱跟着龙走
知道它并没有醒来
大了才想到，舞龙是人见人爱的战争沙盘
所幸盛装的龙，仍未被鞭炮惊醒

## the dragon

what dragons were to begin with doesn't matter anymore
as long as they make the festival germinate in spring
as long as some hearts are gratified when the dragon dances
as long as when there's slush on the ground you can wear
  your new shoes for the new year
as long as when the door of your home creaks open
  it's like seeing long-lost eyes again
giving them the searching gaze of deep emotion

wind has ushered in holiday fragrance
the dragon's on the streets, postage-stamped with
  firecracker smoke
hopeful people sending their peace prayers towards
  the new year

from what were beast's eyes, a thread of confusion shows
  through the smoke
is it the custom to manufacture gladness from explosives?
can a year in the life just passing
be summed up in thunder?

when i was small i liked to trail behind the dragon
knowing that it wouldn't wake
only when i grew up did i realize that the dance
  was everyone's war game
luckily the firecrackers haven't yet roused, in all his regalia,
  the dragon

## 蚂蚁

它像穿铠甲的古代士兵
向我冲来，打算刺上一剑？
它厚重的铠甲里，也灌满一颗心的忧伤？
阳光是金色的手指，在摸索那颗心？

我做不了这样的蚂蚁
无法涉水时牺牲自己，成全蚂蚁群的生机
我是想弄清为何活着的那一只

我把那只蚂蚁堵了很久
想让它感受，活着就是无奈之事
我把那只蚂蚁堵了很久
看它会不会像我一样忧伤？

## the ant

like an ancient warrior in armor
it charges at me—to run me through with its sabre?
does its thick armor cover, too, a sorrowful heart?
is sunlight a golden finger, groping for that heart?

i could never be such an ant
could never sacrifice myself to ford a river, for the
    colony's good
i'd be the ant wondering what life is for

for a long time i blocked the ant's path
wanting it to feel how life is exasperation
for a long time i blocked the ant's path
to see, would that make it sorrowful, like me?

## 白口罩

—2020年春天札记

它像一只素手，突然捂住我的脸
已两个月，我仍不适应
它焐暖我叹息的拥抱
我说出的母语，也应该被它好好过滤？

它是舌头的牢门，关住了多少大言不惭
它让爱情，也不要靠得太近
它说我们的嘴像伤口，需要它来紧紧包扎
它像白月亮那样，让我在梦中埋下一点奢望

它是今春开得最盛的白花
试图与悲伤的颜色相称
它也是病人肺里的冬天
想在众人的脸上长久结冰
让我戴着口罩抱怨时，像含着满口的愧疚

## white mask

*a note from spring 2020*

it's like a white hand, suddenly covering my face
two months already and still not used to it
warm over my sighing embrace
i guess even my mother tongue is carefully filtered

it's the jail gate of the tongue, imprisoning how much hot air
it keeps even love at a distance
it says our mouths are like wounds it needs to
  tightly bandage
it's like a white moon makes me bury my desires in a dream

it's this spring's most abundant white blossom
trying to match the color of grief
it's also winter in a patient's lungs
freezing to permafrost on everyone's faces
and when i complain while masked my mouth fills
  with shame

## 花瓶

花瓶里有心事的深渊
它是花枝临终时的家
花瓶把剪下的花枝，摆成屋里的春天
每一枝都在照看孤单

太安静了，花瓶里的漆黑
也是望着我的黑眼睛
它和花朵的头颅一起垂下，哀悼。
它和花朵的枯容一起衰老，成仙。

花朵，被花瓶高举着
那不是哀求，是能震慑我的室内晚霞
花朵用它死时的大笑，帮我稳住昨天的心情
慰藉我今天再次庸碌的生活

我把花瓶看作花朵的农场
花朵渐渐发黄，是在准备果实累累的金秋？
或者，我把花朵看作花瓶的哨兵
它盯着我在屋里踱步的脚
警惕我踱出的路，会有非分的野心

## vase

a vase holds the heart's depths
flower's home at death's approach
cut posies, arranged for indoor springtime
every stalk ministers to loneliness

too quiet, the vase's pitch
gazes too into my pitch-dark eye
along with the blooms, it bows its head, grieves
along with the blooms, it grows old, sage

the blooms, uplifted by the vase
not in entreaty, but to overawe my indoor sunset
flowers use their time of death for outright laughter,
  easing my own feelings of days past
to console me for another today of life in mediocrity

to me, a vase is a flower farm
the yellow blooms, harbingers for a fertile, a golden autumn?
or maybe the blooms are the vase's sentinel
scrutinizing my pacing in the room
cautioning that my ambitious road
might prove too big for my boots

## 小路

小路沿着围墙，独自遁入林中
它要逃离窗户的眼睛？
它要聆听知了试吹的号角？
它要到林中，带回一只迷途的狗？

哗哗的风，让树都弯着身子恭迎它
它在林中越走越消瘦
脚印和落叶是它的主食
它用越来越细的毛线，护住山的脖子
翻过悬崖时，它凝视着人类的惨剧

它忍受着秋天这张黄疸的脸
向戴着山岚假发的峰顶走去
谁也不知，它究竟要干什么？

当黑夜来临
它成了月光下蛰伏的一条眼镜蛇
慢慢在山顶昂起头——

莫非它自不量力，想给
挥着月亮银盾的黑夜，致命一击？

## the path

the path hugs the enclosure wall, then slips alone
    into the woods
to escape the window's eye?
to hear the cicada's tentative blast?
to meander into the woods and bring back a lost dog?

the rustling wind bows the tree down to reverence it
the more it walks the skinnier it gets
it feeds mostly on footprints, on fallen leaves
winding thread that thins and thins, it shields
    the mountain's neck
it clambers up cliffs, stares transfixed at the human tragedy

enduring autumn's jaundiced visage
it heads to the mist-wigged peak
no one divines its real intentions

when dark night falls
it becomes a cobra coiled watchful in the moonlight
slowly raising its head on the mountaintop

could it be that, prizing itself too highly, it aims to
strike, against night's silver-shield moon,
a lethal blow?

## 致裴多菲

我在博物馆的墙上，见到你的诗
我去布达佩斯的书店，买你的诗
不懂匈牙利文，是我的一种病
我靠把影子投向你的诗，来徒劳地治疗

你的诗寂然无声，它只是听着
我的英文在和店员的英文打架
那一天的人民币在和福林讨价还价
取下诗集，才发现
书架上空出了你向我致意的眼睛

如今，已无少时读你诗的快意
是因为世故已深入骨髓
好在我尚有不懂匈牙利文的病
我要像盲人，用日复一日的抚摸
感受每个字的意味，直到它们在梦里熠熠生辉

## to petőfi

on museum walls, i saw your poems
in that budapest bookstore, i bought your poems
i suffer from the malady of not knowing hungarian
i treat it in vain by casting my shadow over your poems

your poetry is soundless, mute, it just listens
my english battles with the shop clerk's english
on that day when the yuan haggled with the forint
only when i got the book did i notice
your gaze out of the new gap in the bookshelf

i no longer get youthful elation from your poems
since worldliness has seeped into my bones
but at least i still am sick with not knowing hungarian
and like a blind man, i'll use each day's caress
to feel each word's meaning, until they gleam in my dreams

## 约会

我等着和她会面
我打开一本书——

突然，形容词散发着她的体香
动词留下了她的脚印
名词带来她的安静

那一刻，那本书就是怯生生的她

## date

i’m waiting for my date with her
i open a book—

suddenly, the adjectives give forth her scent
the verbs leave her footprints
the nouns carry her quietude

at that moment, the book is, timidly, her

## 孤独

孤独不会变异
它在古代，就已经古老

我走过一棵古树
用手摸着巨大的根
我的孤独
竟扎得像树根一样深
惊动了田鼠的睡眠

## solitude

solitude doesn't alter
in ancient times it was ancient already

i passed an ancient tree
felt its enormous trunk
my solitude
is deep like tree roots
and startles the sleeping vole

## 夜行火车

雨像彻夜不歇的马蹄
它敲打的褐色土地彻夜不醒

一块褐土的皮肤上，一列火车正驰过
我瞥见车窗里的倩影，仿佛一根华丽的羽毛
火车报答了做梦的皮肤

## night train

rain like hooves unsleeping through the night
hammers the brown earth unwaking through the night

over the brown skin of soil a train is just passing
i glimpse a beauty through the train windows,
    like a stunning feather
the train rewards the dreaming skin

## 集体舞

我们手拉手
围住一只高脚凳
凳上什么也没有
我们的手上除了手
什么也没有

## group dance

we hold hands
and dance around a high stool
on the stool is nothing
in our hands there is nothing
except hands

# 玉

你的肩上背着皇帝
你一放下，一个朝代就崩塌了

你的耳里，满是太监的尖叫
你想远行的双脚，长在宫女迈不出宫的腿上

你是皇帝掌心的月亮
照亮过宫廷的每个阴谋

你是没有骨头的骨头
没有色彩的色彩

没有人知道，你肌肤如丝
舌头却冰如刺刀

jade

you carry the emperor on your shoulders
and when you let him off, the dynasty collapses

ringing always in your ears—the shrieks of eunuchs
your feet want to take you far away, but are stuck to the legs
    of palace maidens who can never leave

you are the moon in the emperor's palm
glowing to reveal all the palace plots

you are boneless bone
colourless colour

no one knows your silken skin
but blade-cold tongue

## 思念

奶奶手上的那碗白米饭
如今，端在我的手上

每一粒都成为我胃里思念的风暴
每一粒都穿过我羞愧的肠道
奔回大地——
现在，思念伸展在无垠的稻田
密密地立成稻杆

## longing

that bowl of rice in grandma's hand
i am now holding in mine

every grain has become a storm of longing in my stomach
every grain has passed through my shameful gut
rushing to the great soil—
now longing reaches through the boundless paddies
turning to dense rice sprouts

## 河蚌

用手掰开河蚌
这就是人主动上门的拜访？
读书人，已不上门找书

对着河蚌掰开的嘴
人要的，不是可以对话的舌头
人要的，是一场河蚌的苦难

人配得上河蚌的赴死？
配得上河蚌托付的未来？
人走得出河蚌闭眼的黑暗？

河蚌的余生，本该在流水潺潺的河畔
本会聆听，老人打盹儿的鼾声
春天的寂静，本来是另一场灾难

吞下河蚌的人，貌似慈悲
起身去禅寺祈福
学会遗忘的智慧

## freshwater clam

prying open a clam
is that what you call paying a visit?
scholars don't visit for books anymore

facing the clam's pried-open mouth
what humans want isn't a tongue that can dialogue
what humans want is the suffering of the clam

are people worth the death of clams?
worth the future the clams entrust us?
can people find a way out of the darkness caused by
    the closed eye?

the clam should have spent the rest of the babble
    at the riverbank
it should have been listening to the snores of
    an old man dozing
the solitude of spring ought to be a separate disaster

the people who swallow the clam seem compassionate
they get up and pray for good fortune at the zen temple
to learn the wisdom of forgetfulness

## 踏青

我在家中读书，窗外雾霭沉沉
冬雪之后，来了几日暖风
梅花红了，有炊烟飘在山岭处……

邀上几位朋友，悄悄上路
不知春天将教会谁什么？
随便什么花，都够人消磨
孤独，还是那么辽阔……

古道险峻得像是爱情
隔着山寺，我的心跟着一只风筝摇晃
太阳变红时，有人站在山顶在听
连出洞的蝙蝠，也知道此时应该闭上嘴巴

## spring excursion

reading at home, heavy mist through the window
after the winter snows, we've now had a few days
    of warm wind
red plum blossoms, kitchen smoke over the
    mountain peaks…

got a couple friends together, set quietly off
who knows what spring will teach, or whom
any flowers will do for the idle
and solitude remains just as vast…

old paths steep like love
beyond the temple my heart sways with that kite
when the sun reddens, someone on the peak listens to
the bats flitting from the cave, knows enough to shut up

## 家乡

那年九月，远方对准了我的心
我离家，走外省，该是多么不孝
路途爱上的小溪，都没有名字
钟山既实实在在，又像假的——

要抛下家乡的龙王山，并不容易
一样的毛竹，激起的心事各不相同
一样的寂静，也散着不一样的含蓄
我感慨钟山时，偏像感慨着龙王山

后来，家乡并不适宜回去——
拆掉的古镇，在心中空出的是黑暗
有一年，我想通了，为什么来外省
我只剩一个旧的家乡，和它不能再生离死别
现在，家乡仿佛就是我自己……

## hometown

that year's september, distance took aim at my heart
i left home, left the province, such an undutiful son
the river i fell in love with—nameless for the whole trip
bell mountain seemed tangible, and also a fake—

casting off dragon king mountain, near home, was far
from easy
the same moso bamboo raked up completely
different emotions
the same silence, though exuding a different subtlety
and each sigh for bell mountain seemed to be a sigh
for dragon king mountain

later on, it didn't make sense to go home—
the old town was razed, and what took its place in my heart
was darkness
this one year i figured out why i had left my home province
to come here
i only have a former hometown, from which i cannot
separate
and now it seems i am my own hometown

## 繁体与简体

繁体适合返乡，简体更适合遗忘
繁体葬着我们的祖先，简体已被酒宴埋葬
繁体像江山，连细小的灰尘也要收集
简体像书包，不愿收留课本以外的东西
繁体扇动着无数的翅膀，但不发出一点噪声
简体却像脱缰之马，只顾驰骋在乱发脾气的平原
当繁体搀扶着所有走得慢的名词和形容词
简体只顾建造动词专用的高铁

简体会说，繁体长得像半死不活的碑文
会讥讽，繁体还穿着旗袍、蹬着三寸金莲、戴着民国的假睫毛
会把繁体的安静、低调，说成是不善辞令
会把自己脸上的色斑，说成是福痣
当繁体把话题交给上半身
简体的梦已卡在下半身，无法拔出
忙碌中，简体像雾气，从不想排队
繁体相信，排队的耐心能造一把好斧子，能写一本好哲学

## full-form and simplified

full-form suits homecoming, simplified suits forgetting
full-form inters our ancestors, simplified has already been
buried in banquets
full-form is like the rivers and hills, gathering in even
the tiniest speck of dust
simplified is like a schoolbag, only textbooks are permitted
full-form flaps its countless wings, yet never makes the
slightest sound
simplified is like an unleashed horse, it just wants to gallop
across the furious plain
while full-form helps along all the slow-moving nouns
and adjectives
simplified only cares about building high-speed railways
for verbs

simplified would say that full-form is like the moribund
epigraphy of steles,
would mock full-form, still dressed in its red mandarin
gown, with its three-inch lotus feet and the Republic's
fake eyelashes
would call the calmness, the subtlety of full-form—
failures of rhetoric
would call the freckles on its own face—beauty spots
and while the full-form leads the conversation to higher parts
simplified's imagination is caught below the belt, can never
be unstuck
when things get busy, simplified is like fog, unwilling to
wait its turn
full-form believes that the patience of waiting its turn might
sharpen a hardy axe, might inspire a wise philosophy

简体已砍去多少枝条，就已留下多少伤口
繁体每多一道弯，就多一条路
就多了前世和来世，不像简体，只能把自己捐给今生
瞧，简体把最重的担子已卸给繁体，生怕被快乐抛弃
但简体不知，繁体身上的锈迹，也是夺目的鳞片
繁体身上的寂静，也是动人的歌声
当我，被夹在繁体和简体之间
我就像最后一个知情者，日夜承受着秘密的负重

how many twigs and branches has simplified hacked off,
  how many wounds has it left behind
with each extra hook of full-form's brush, another road
  opens to
the world before and the world to come, not like simplified,
  which only ever endows itself upon the now
see, simplified has already unloaded the heaviest burden on
  full-form, lest contentment abandon it
but simplified doesn't know that even the marks of rust on
  full-form's body are actually dazzling scales
the loneliness of full-form, too, is a touching song
and when i get stuck between full-form and simplified
then i am like the last person to know the truth, bearing
  day and night this secret, heavy burden

# Huang Fan

Wang Ping Translations

## 鱼

像灯一样的眼，为什么没有照亮？
像花蕾一样的眼，为什么没有盛开？
莫非你也像人一样，一直戴着面具？
为什么你有足够多的骨头
偏到死后才试图卡住人的喉咙？

我守着装你的盘子
守着怜你的假慈悲
你散发的浓香，来自你血腥的死亡
你一生的故事，我吃进嘴里还有用么？
你一生的视野，我用舌头也能继承么？

想到你是一个生命，甚至鱼里的先知
我不再是瞎子和聋子
一刹那，我成了能听懂你遗言的罪人

## Fish

Your eyes shine like lamps, why can't they light up
  anything?
Your eyes bulge like buds, why don't they blossom?
Are you like humans also wearing a mask?
With your abundant bones
Why do you wait till you're dead to choke us?

I guard the plate that holds your body
Guarding my fake compassion for you
Your delicious smell comes from your bloody death
Who would tell your story once it enters my mouth?
How would my tongue inherit your vision?

Once I realize you are part of life, a fish prophet
I'm no longer blind or deaf
Suddenly, I become a sin that understands your last words.

## 流水

校园里，抽水机让水翻着跟头
它把死水的霉床单，掀起来晒太阳
秋风一样路过的师生
不认为扬得高高的水，与他们有关

几个农民工，直直盯着流水
没有谁的眼神比他们更贪婪
流水窘得低下头
埋进河沟这道深深的伤口

还是秋天，他们已谈论冬天
是因为流水中有火，能让水不结冰？
是因为扬得高高的水，像农民干活弓着背？
是因为流水用锦绣的白棉花，催促他们还乡？

抽水机把一匹水的白马，拴在身边
只有农民工听见，它嘶鸣的求救声——
师生的冷眼是刀子，割得它疼啊

一个农民工，把脸低到马脚下
让脸上的尘土，扎入流水一起还乡

## Flowing Water

On the campus, a pump sends water into somersaults
Peeling the moldy sheet from dead water to hang in the sun
Students and professors pass by like autumn wind
No one gives a second thought to the splashing water

A few peasant workers stare at the water
Such greedy looks in their eyes
Embarrassed water buries its face under their gaze
A wound buried deep in the running ditch

It's still autumn, but the workers are already talking
 about winter
Is it because the fire in the flowing water stops it
 from freezing?
Or the splashing water bends like a working peasant's back?
Or because the water foams like cotton, calling them home?

The water pump ties water to its side like a white horse
Only the migrant workers hear its neighing for help
The campus' indifferent eyes cut deep into its flesh

A peasant worker lowers his face to the horse's hooves
The dust on his face joins in the water flowing all
 the way home

## 河蚌

用手掰开河蚌
这就是人主动上门的拜访？
读书人，已不上门找书

对着河蚌掰开的嘴
人要的，不是可以对话的舌头
人要的，是一场河蚌的苦难

人配得上河蚌的赴死？
配得上河蚌托付的未来？
人走得出河蚌闭眼的黑暗？

河蚌的余生，本该在流水潺潺的河畔
本该聆听，老人打盹儿的鼾声
春天的寂静，本来是另一场灾难

吞下河蚌的人，貌似慈悲
起身去禅寺祈福
学会遗忘的智慧

## Clam

Opening the clam with hands
Is this a mankind's knocking for a visit?
But intellectuals no longer seek books

Facing the clam's force-opened mouth
Mankind no longer wants the tongue for a dialogue
They want clam's pain

Is mankind worthy of clam's martyrdom?
Are we worthy of the future the clam delivered to us?
Can we walk out of the dark in its closed eye?

Clam is supposed to live in a running river
Supposed to listen to old men's snores
The silent spring is supposed to be another disaster

The man who swallowed the clam looks kind-hearted
As he rises to pray in a temple
And learns the wisdom of forgetting

## 运奴船

——观特纳油画有感

他们把黑人像一网鱼，装入船舱
黑人是那么驯服
沉默成了黑人安慰自己的口香糖
身上的脂肪，成了熬过航程的唯一希望

那么多的黑人，像鱼饵
被抛入大海，用血的光芒
照亮海水，直到鲨鱼的唇上
沾满黑人的临终遗言

假如我也是黑奴，必定会重复
那种尖叫的命运，我的皮
也一定是黑夜的皮，我的血
也一定是美术馆中最贵的血
但在鲨鱼休战之前，我只能幻想
爬出一排排牙齿的铁栅

观完《运奴船》，我也试着
掂一掂自己的命运。我恍然大悟——
自己已是城市的黑奴
在欲望休战之前，已没有谁能帮我

## Slave Ship

*after Turner's painting*

They boarded Africa onto the ship, like a net of fish
The slaves seemed docile
Chewing silence like bubblegum
Their body fat was the only hope to survive this voyage

And so many of them were tossed
Like bait, into the waves
Their blood lit up the sea, their last cry
Hung on the jaws of sharks

If I were a slave, would I repeat
That screaming destiny, my skin
Darker than night, my blood
Reaching the highest bid in a museum?
As sharks finish their feeding frenzy
I can only imagine crawling through the steel fence's teeth

After the "Slave Ship," I try to weigh my own fate—
How heavy it is. And I realize
I have been a slave to the city
Nobody can save me from the war of desire

## 玫瑰为我脸红

每支玫瑰都有一对红脸颊
在为我脸红
我只顾戴好口罩，走进重霾的冬日
只顾活着，等着世间的不幸自己消瘦
看见污水的斑斓色泽，却说那是蝴蝶复活

玫瑰，水一样漫进梦中
在为我脸红
我踏上的路，通向衣锦荣华
我只是看着卖艺的老翁，一贫如洗
只是和那么多的人，从他的哀伤里路过

那么多的劫难，和我挤在同一个时代
我却只想躲得远远的
是啊，我再也成不了谁的依靠了
只有玫瑰谴责我
在为我脸红

## Rose Is Blushing for Me

Every rose has a pair of rosy cheeks
They blush for me
As I put on my mask, before walking into winter's smog
I live to be alive, wasting away amidst the world's
misfortunes
Butterflies resurrect in sewage rainbow colors

Roses seep into my dreams like water
Blushing for me
I've chosen a path towards fame and riches
I watch the old artist selling on streets, not a penny
to his name
I walk past his misery, like every other passerby

So many disasters share the crowded era with me
All I want is to hide, get away as far as possible
True, nobody can depend on me any more
Only the rose is watching
Blushing for me

## 出血的眼睛

左眼出血，黑瞳仁
像架在火上烧的黑煤
右眼看着春天的灾难，仿佛说
是哭的时候了，请试着用泪
浇灭眼中的大火

医生叫我闭着眼。关上眼皮的炉门
炉火就不会灼伤内心？
眼里的红色，是想长成红玫瑰的红旗？
眼里的红灯，是想拦下不戴口罩的行人？
眼里的红火，是想把瞳仁的黑，锻成淬蓝？

我的眼里，何尝不是火星的红尘？
那样的文明，早已下落不明
莫非，那样的红尘已盯上地球？
我闭上眼，宁愿让黑夜在眼里升起
宁愿让左眼的泪，在脸上修一条
绕开舌头的运河

## Bleeding Eyes

My left eye is bleeding, black pupil
Burning like coal on fire
My right eye watches the spring's disaster, as if saying
It's time to cry, to put out the fire
With your tears

My doctor told me to close my eyelids, furnace door
 to my eyes
Would that prevent fire from scorching my heart?
Is the blood in my eyes trying to become a rose-colored flag?
Is the red light in my eyes trying to stop the
 maskless pedestrians?
Is the fire in my eyes trying to forge the black pupil
 into blue?

My eyes once contained red dust from the Mars
A lost civilization
Could it be true that the red planet is eyeing the earth?
I close my lids, let night rise in my eyes
Let my tears in my left eye run on my cheek
To open a canal, away from my tongue

## 灯

你喜欢买灯，仿佛已厌倦太阳
喜欢灯在夜里，伸出黄皮肤的手臂
喜欢它抚摸，铺在床上的睡梦
唯有黑夜才让你看清，光线该有多干净！

灯的手，能被你回忆的泪打湿吗？
它用干净的手指，要取出你揉进眼里的沙子？
你不敢正眼看灯，是因为你有太多的愧疚？
灯把手伸向门缝，是在操心门外的黑暗？

一整夜，灯用铜链，把你拴在桌前
你写下的每个字，都有春天的夜色
你甚至希望，白天与黑夜永远分居
直到天亮，你才看清
夜里的迷人光线，原来都来自灯泡的灰头土脸

## Lamps

You like to buy lamps, as if you were tired of the sun
You like to reach out at night, your yellow arms
Stroking the dreams sprawled in bed
Only darkness shows how clean the light can be

Would your memory's tears soak the lamp's hand?
Could its clean fingers clear the dust in your eyes?
You would not look at the lamp. Is it lit because you carry
too much guilt?
The lamp reaches into the door's crack. Is it worrying
about the night outside?

All night long, the lamp chains you to the desk with
bronze shackles
Every word you write carries the color of spring
You even hope to separate days and nights forever
Till dawn arrives, and you realize
The shimmering beauty throughout the night came from
a dusty light bulb

## 三文鱼

题记：新闻报道，北欧三文鱼的养殖环境恶劣，
鱼虱泛滥成灾，病鱼身上布满溃疡------

我不想再打听什么
三文鱼身上的大块溃疡，已说明一切
人在北欧，与人在东亚，又有什么区别？
鱼一生的痛，只是人看见溃疡的冷漠一瞥

人对自己的溃疡，从不歌唱
却把滋生溃疡的鱼池，唱成三文鱼的天堂
苦难的鱼，也有幻想登天的宗教么？
也会像人用学问，把溃疡说成磨难中的希望？

鱼虱把它的登山镐，牢牢钉在鱼皮上
让鱼习惯，那些叮咬的痛是鱼虱掐捏的爱情
那些爱抒情的人，也会把个人的厄运
看成春情的浪漫？

我小时的身躯，也曾停泊在虱子的港湾
虱子的勤奋劳作，让我的睡眠碎得像沙
哪怕用一周的睡眠，也拼不出一个完整的梦
有谁会俯下身，也哄一哄鱼的睡眠？

鱼池已经蓄满人的恶
它也会溢出，把人养在更大的池中

## Salmon

*on Norwegian salmon farms, where fish in crowded ponds are covered with sores from lice*

I don't need to know more
Those sores on salmon said everything
Humans in Northern Europe, humans in Eastern Asia—
 same difference?
The pain in salmon's life is just another indifferent glance

We never celebrate our own sores
But we sing those crowded farms as if they were paradise
Poor salmon, do they pray for a religion where
 heaven exists?
Would they turn their sores into hope through endless pain?

Lice hang on salmon's skin like Black Diamond Raven Axes
They make salmon believe their pain is just a lover's grip
 or pinch
The way some lyrical poets romanticize
Their own ill fate, trauma, agony

My childhood body was once parked in a lice bay
Their diligent work ground my sleep into grains of sand
A week's sleep can't complete a single dream
Now who will bend over and sing a lullaby to the
 sleepless salmon?

The fish pond is brimming with evil
Soon it'll overflow, spilling humans into a bigger pond

## 野猫

每天傍晚，那只野猫就像夜色
悄悄来临，它没有苟且偷生的低贱
它用优雅的步态穿过苦难，走向我
它不像人，会把脚步声走得像歌声

它没有让人劳神的名字
身上的绒毛，比任何名字更可靠
它用隐士身份，配合着这漫漫长夜
我撒下的猫粮，能把它的命运拖入小康？

我的施舍里，到底有多少真心？
也许这施舍，只是抵御虚无的一种风情
在黑夜打烊之前，就连星星的酒窝也不真实

多么香啊！它的吃相是银行
一样存着人类的饥馑
它浓密的绒毛，也像人类的棉衣
一样有着过冬的警觉

我用口哨，打造着它和我的方言
每一声，都是一粒憧憬

## Stray Cat

At dusk, that stray cat would arrive
Quiet like night, no appearance of hunger or struggle
It crosses the suffering in elegance towards me
Unlike humans, each step strikes up a song

It doesn't have a name to confuse my thoughts
Its fur is more trustworthy than any names
Like a hermit, it collaborates with long nights
Would the food I put out lift its fate into the middle class?

My charity, how much of it comes from the heart?
Maybe it's just a gesture to fight great emptiness
Before night closes its door, nothing is true, not even dimples on a star

Look at her appetite! She eats in the manner of
A bank, saving all the hunger of humanity
Her coat is thick like winter jackets
Warning of the coming winter

I whistle, to build our common tongue
Each sound is a grain of longing

## 雷

小时，总怕被雷击中
曾有几次，雷追得我满地跑
奶奶说，雷下面的树是油库
你是火柴，千万别靠近树

天晴了，我也不敢接受树的好意
仍担心雷还活着。树不是雷的裹脚布？
树叶的沙沙声，不是雷的充电声？
兴许心里一直有雷声，我才把童身
留到二十五岁

现在，雷是刺入梦里的刺刀
梦中的钢板，对它无效
它常朝我的噩梦，连开数枪
让我在春天醒来，却不敢动弹

它的怒声，是给乱世穿上的新衣
当我老了，忘了从前的人与事
它会急忙折回，用暴烈的坏脾气
大声告诉我！

## Thunder

As a child, I was terrified of thunder
Many times, it chased me around
Nana said: trees under thunder are oil reserves
And you are a match, so don't get close to trees

When the sun came out, I still hesitated to accept trees'
good will
Still wondered if thunder was alive, if trees were cloths
binding thunder's feet
If that rustling was the sound of thunder charging
their power
Maybe the thundering noise in my heart preserved
my virginity
Till I reached 25.

Now the thunder has become a bayonet into my dreams
Where even steel is useless against its attacks
It opens fires at my nightmares
Rendering me paralyzed when I awaken in spring

Their angry roars are clothes, covering cities and
villages' shame
In the rain, their scolding noises bury the troubled times
When I get old and start forgetting things and people
They will rush back, to remind me
With their thunderous temper!

## 虎

它就是酷夏，一靠近它
你的汗，就开始荡洗衣服
你的勇气，随靠近它的距离
一寸一寸缩短

饲养员把它锁在铁笼里
但威胁，照样穿过铁笼扑向你
你活得五光十色，却逃不出它目光的鞭挞——
你不过活在衣服的节日里，金钱的荒凉中

它在笼中的高视阔步，永远令你回味
你纵有千里江山可以行走
脚下却只剩一条路
你甚至不敢，邀它一起挥霍

在它咄咄的逼视下，你仿佛正成为被告

## Tiger

He is the mid-summer, as soon as you get close
Your sweat begins to pour over your clothes
Your courage gets shorter inch by inch
As you get closer

The zoo keeper locks him in the steel cage
But the threat lunges at you through the steely bars
Your life may be glorious, but you still can't escape the
    whipping of his eyes
You only live in the festival of shopping, in the waste land
    of money

He strides in the cage, and you realize
Even if you got thousands of rivers and mountains to choose
    for your travel
Your only path lies under your feet
And you dare not invite him to squander it with you
Under his gaze, you feel you're becoming a defendant

## 偏头痛

头痛时，是谁在我体内发脾气？
已经二十年，我还未弄懂它的用语——
身子要躺下，眼睛要闭上
嘴还要像工地，发出嘈杂声

身子蜷缩的样子，像要回到子宫
莫非我年过半百，仍需要定期回炉？
或像疲惫的帆，需要把自己再次折叠？

头上的痛像鼓点，不停敲打
风来到窗口，要合奏一支流行曲？
痛让舌头抱住呻吟
不让呻吟展开翅膀

痛是大海，让我看到了日子的风景
痛在怪我，还不懂去菜场买菜的幸福？
当痛临近，连过去的落寞也是满足
我的痛并不孤单，一本历史书
就是一座收藏疼痛的博物馆

## Migraine

And here it comes, throwing a tantrum in my body
20 years already, I still don't know its language
The body has to lie down, the eyes must close
The mouth, like a construction site, utters piercing sounds

The body curls, wishing to return to the womb
I've lived 50 years on the earth, do I need a rebirth?
Maybe I'm just a battered boat, wishing to fold and
  unfold my sail?

The migraine beats me like a drum, non-stop
Wind knocking on the window, does it want to join in for
  a pop song?
Pain ties my tongue around moaning
Forbidding it to open its wings

Pain is a sea, showing me the horizon of life
Pain scolds me for not knowing the joy of a farmer's market
When pain approaches, even past loneliness
  becomes content
My pain is no longer alone; it has become a history book
A museum that collects suffering

## 木梯

梯子把我变成鸽子，让我在楼顶眺望
对我在高处的誓言，梯子沉默不语
梯子也听着风的动人话语，对风许诺的远方
并不折腰感谢

每次爬梯子，我都忍不住找它的眼睛
我会一脚踩瞎它的眼吗？
每块踏板，是它让我跳舞的广场吗？
我用一生的负重，压住了它交心的舌头？

梯子让我更接近天意了
我活动双臂，是为了更适合飞翔？
我察看天空，是想知道
昨晚的雷声，来自哪个神的愤怒？

梯子把牙齿，永远埋在被我踩踏的沉默里
把它的森林故乡，藏在我对远方的眺望中

## Ladder

The ladder turns me into a pigeon, looking out from
the tower
I make a pledge from the top, but the ladder keeps quiet
And refuses to bend over in gratitude
As it listens to wind's sweet whispers, its promise of
a distant place

When I climb the ladder, I can't help but look for its eyes
Would I blind it with my misstep?
Can I dance on each of its rungs as if on a park square?
Am I pressing too hard on its J-lock tongue with the weight
of my life?

The ladder lifts me closer to Providence
I wave my arms, preparing for a flight?
I look around at the sky, wondering
which angry god roared through last night's thunder

The ladder buries its teeth in silence, under my feet
Its forest home forever hidden in my distant gaze

## 梅雨

这是独属于东北亚的雨
发霉是这个雨季的主要矿藏
它让我最信任的诺言，也长满霉斑
我捧起的历史书，已潮得滴得下泪水

空气用它蘸水的毛巾，擦拭我的脸
它想擦掉我的面具，看到里面的心
连灰尘，也学会含泪的舞蹈
来配合梅雨一年一度的呢喃

那些灯下的人影，也在出汗啊
连我的叹息，也闪着汗粒
和我一起忍受，梅雨的桑拿浴
洗得湿淋淋的日子，会比过去干净吗？

如果风能吹干诺言、人影、叹息、历史
它们会留下一层盐粒么？
尝一尝，会有血的咸味么？

## Plum Rain

It belongs to northeast Asia
Mold becomes the main element in the rainy season
It spreads its rings onto my most trusted promise
I pick up my history book, so wet it rains teardrops

Air wipes my face with its wet towel
Erasing my mask to look into the heart
Even dust has learned its tearful dance
To match the murmuring season of the plum rain

And the shadows under the lamp are also sweating
Even my sighs, dripping with sweat
Who'd endure with me this plum rain sauna?
Would life be cleaner, having soaked in the rain?

If wind dries up promises, shadows, sighs and history
Would they leave behind some grains of salt?
Would they keep some salty taste of blood?

# 水平仪

水平仪的眼睛，噙满泪水
谁是里面那个空虚的气泡
从不愿意坐在中央
宁愿水平仪，有一只俾倪的眼睛

当少年用木刨，刨出令人心动的桌面
他盼着水平仪，能正眼看他
但他不知，它的眼里只有空空的行囊
装满对大海起伏的向往

他也不知，水平仪无法闭眼的悲伤——
哪怕一只蚂蚁的苦难，也会涌入眼睛
甚至涌入中东枪弹呼啸的黑暗

就算盯着水平仪，他也不懂
俾倪，是它坚持了一生的宿命

## The Level

Its eyes are filled with tears
What's that empty bubble
Never willing to sit in the middle
Why does it look at me, always askance?

When the boy cuts the table with a wood planer
How he wishes the leveler would look at him straight
He has no idea this eye is empty of baggage
Filled with wonder, sailing in the sea

He's not aware of its sorrow, unable to close its eye—
Even an ant's pain can seep in
And flying bullets in the dark from the Middle East

He won't understand, no matter how long he stares:
It lives because of its askance stance

## 吻

少年时，我曾想要一个吻
认定吻，是铺向幸福的一条路
春天了，当少女们穿上裙子
我的吻，却只在书中绽开

恋爱的日子来临，吻
成了打开身体的一个习俗
我在吻中眺望，却望不见未来
求生一样的吻声，不再是少年布道的祷词

结婚多年以后，偶尔会在吻中
听见婚姻破裂的声音
吻也像生活，渐渐平淡无趣
吻也像工作，成了一种苦行

现在，我不再有吻了
但有工作和生活
窗外一只布谷鸟的叫声
一首旧歌的乐曲声，只有它们还在操心
该如何安顿一个少年的吻

## Kiss

I longed for a kiss in my teenage years
I believed it would pave my path to happiness
Spring came, and girls wore skirts
My kiss opened only in books

When the day of love arrived, kissing
Became a habit to open the body
I looked out in the middle of action, but saw no future
My kiss sounded more like survival than my teenage prayer

After years of marriage, I hear
Sounds of breaking in an occasional kiss
Like life, kissing became flat and routine
Like work, it became an ascetic journey

No more kisses for me now
Only work and life
Outside my window, a cuckoo is singing
An old song, still worrying
How to settle a teenager's kiss

## 走路

走路时，鞋子一直沙沙叫疼
我装作那是祝福
想到走路会把健康带给虚无
我就装聋作哑

路边的树叶也哗哗哗
是为鞋子叫苦，还是为秋天唱着颂歌？
沙子是一群发怒的牛，用犄角顶着鞋的斗篷
也许没有伤口，才是沙子一生的痛苦

鞋子，是抱怨我的中年越来越重？
是用沙沙声，替我为生活咳嗽？
我给鞋子的每克压力，也是给大地的一克苦难？
我感激鞋子，配上风的乐曲，把什么都唱出来

走再远的路，都差一个终点把我留住
只有家，刚好可以放下我的牵挂
我从未发胖，也许身体怀着对鞋子的愧疚
用恒定的体重，道出对鞋子的珍惜

## Walking

When I walk, my shoes squeak in pain
I pretend it's a blessing
Walking will take my health to void
So I pretend to not hear the pain

The leaves on the roadsides are rustling
Are they moaning for my shoes? Or just singing for autumn?
Sand is a raging bull, his horns against the red capes of
  my shoes
Maybe sand feels the pain, when there's no more wound

Shoes, are you moaning about my heavy middle age?
Are you coughing for my life, through your grinding teeth?
Each ounce of pressure under my step adds pain to the earth
But I'm grateful how you turn pain into songs, using wind
  as your melody

No matter where I've traveled, there's no destination to
  keep me there
Only home, just the right size for my thoughts and worries
I haven't put on weight all these years, maybe it's my way
To say how much I treasure you, with my fixed weight

## 郊区的辩证法

郊区，让我心如止水
让我熟悉了风的拳头
让我知道了雨对窗户的失望——
我朗朗的读诗声，死死被窗户挡住

世界已面目全非
我的孤独像根，还在悄悄深入
天上沉睡的云，却扭着清醒的舞蹈
它忘了，朝大地撒下影子的黑郁金香

我坐着时，思想比站着高
我躺下时，爱情比坐着多
我盼着像良田，就算披着满身稻子
也不炫耀繁华

我的嗓子，从来就缺一块簧片
无法把中年吹得更响
我也是原地打转的山路，会把天气当药方——
夏天的爱情有湿疹，冬天的思想会干裂

我听着保姆的炒菜声，知道食欲
是多么的不自由，却是美的

## Dialectic of Suburbs

Suburbs calm my heart like still water
They let me know the taste of wind's fist

The world has changed
My loneliness, like roots, digs deeper into silence
The sleeping clouds dance in full awareness
Forgetting to cast black tulip shadows on earth

When I sit, my thoughts stand taller than my height
In bed, my love weighs more than my crouching thoughts
I long to look like the fields, my body hung with rice
But I have no need to show off my glory

My throat lacks a piece of reed
To blow my middle age into a higher tone
I'm a road circling on the mountain, the weather becomes
    my prescription—
In summer, my love turns into eczema, in winter,
    my thoughts crack

The sound of cooking whets my appetite
So restricted, yet so beautiful

## 骑马

去年夏天，我去那拉提骑马
马把头垂下，我在慌张中成了它的主人
要费多大的劲，我才能靠近它那颗奔驰的心？
我夹紧马肚，像一朵乌云，抱着一团风

草原上，哪里有城里人说的那种路？
遍地肥草对马蹄的爱，远甚车轮
甚至期待马蹄再熨一遍它们的夏衣
我被马背，颠成了世上最轻的一个名字

我看不懂蹄印编织的图案
但猜测，那蹄声也有着民歌的疼痛
也许马知道，前方还有一个我该去的地方
但善意的哈族少年让我相信，起点就是终点

## Horse Ride

Last summer, I went to Nalati for a horse ride
The horse bent his head. In a hurry, I became his master
How much effort do I need, to get close to his running heart?
I tightened my legs, holding onto a gust of wind, like a
dark cloud

Where's the city road running on the grassland?
The thick grass loves horse hoofs, far better than wheels
They hope the horses will iron their summer clothes
one more time
The horseback bumped my name down the lightest on earth

I don't know the design woven by his hooves
I can feel the pain in his songs through each of his steps
Maybe the horse knows my destination ahead of us
But the kind Ha boy lets me understand that the beginning
is the end

## 枕头

我埋头在它的怀里
只有我听得见，它唱的催眠曲
只有它理解，我的幸福是作梦
梦里才有冰，给越烘越热的心事降温

我的头是牙齿
清晨给枕头留下坑洼的牙印
枕头像被子，留下照看我一夜的疲惫皱纹

枕头低着头，还在寻找梦中人的地址？
它知道，我心里有哪只邮包
至今还没有寄出？

当我带着梦中的密语醒来
只有枕头理解，我在梦里才不孤单
它和被子用一床的凌乱
替我藏起梦中的心满意足

## Pillow

I bury my head in her bosom
Only I can hear her lullaby
Only she knows my happiness lives in dreaming
And the ice from dreams cools my burning anxiety

My head is teeth
Leaving pothole marks in the morning
Fatigue wrinkles from all night care, like those on
 the blanket

Head bent, is she seeking the address in sleep?
Does she know, which packet
Hasn't been mailed out yet?

When I awaken from the dream code
She knows why my loneliness vanishes from my sleep
Together with the blanket in the unmade bed
They hide my contentment deep in my dream

## 大海

大海是勤奋的运动员
也有着陌生的脾气
它穿上浪的白袜时
海上竟没有一丝脚气

鱼是大海播下的种子
它们像铆钉
把大海的恩情一直铆到海底——
它们很享受这张哗哗摇晃的摇床

人学着像种子，把自己撒入大海
却像刀子，把珊瑚扎出了血
人的幸福，竟是伸入海中的脏舌头
一遍一遍去舔
大海清澈的心

## Ocean

The sea is a hardcore athlete
With a strange temper
It wears white wavy socks
But never suffers athlete's foot

Fish are seeds sowed by the sea
Like rivets
They fasten the ocean love all the way to the bottom—
Then enjoy the loud, rocking cradle

We mirror seeds, diving into the sea
We bleed corals like knives
Our happiness is a filthy tongue,
Licking, licking
Clean
The ocean's heart

## 书房

我可以没有别的，但必须有一间书房
我在里面可以作梦，或者失眠
可以在黄昏，瞥见黑夜如何把白天缴械
窗外的风再猛烈，也搅乱不了我的呼吸

我必须一个人呆着
这古老的孤寂，多么令人安慰啊
令我看出，白墙的所有裂缝
都是一个白头翁的皱纹——
我竭力向他打探，这乐谱吟唱的弦外之音

我常盯着地面，它早已把尘埃当朋友
把我的脚当下棋的棋手
我对它布置的残局，常感到恼火——
它总能算出，我与世界的和解还差几步？

只要书架上的书，还在坚持是非
我在书房就有做不完的事

## Study

I can own nothing but must have a study
Where I can dream or lose my sleep
At dusk, I can watch the day surrender to night
And no wind outside my window can disturb my breathing

I must be alone
How comforting is this ancient loneliness
I can see all the cracks on the white walls
Come from a white-haired man's wrinkles—
I keep begging him to teach me the hidden meaning of music

I stare at the floor that made friends with dust
It checkmates my feet
Annoying me to no end with its endgame--
It always knows how many missteps I have with the world

As long as the books still know right and wrong on
  the shelves
I'll have endless things to do in my studio

《词汇表》续

死亡，人口最多的国家
家，恋人用爱争夺来的抱怨
柏林墙，长在东西之间的白内障
写作，试图用文字叫醒坟墓里的大师
群山，永远晒不黑的动物，数百年才肯移动一步
边缘，再微弱的星光，仍会疏远阳光
骨头，哪怕主人竭力弯腰，它仍坚持挺直的初衷
钥匙，锁的丈夫
恐惧，担心的事，只是还没发生而已
错字，一次逃出字典婚姻的尝试
翻译，总有一些文字，会在异国走失

Word List (continued)

Death: the most populous country
Family: complaining between lovers won with love
Berlin Wall: cataract between East and West
Writing: try to awaken the masters in the graves with words
Mountains: animals that can't be tanned, move one step after hundreds of years
Edge: no matter how weak, the stars still keep their distance
with the sun
Bone: the master wants to bend, but it insists its original uprightness.
Key: lock's husband who loves to get out
Fear: worry about things that are yet to happen
Typo: attempts to escape the marriage of dictionary
Translation: always some words, lost in a foreign land

## 鞋与脚

鞋打算仰望一切
打算把敌人，也看得无比高大
但它仰望不了，永远趴在地上的阴影
甚至不敢看，阴影那双失望的眼
它只好狠心踩过阴影的漫长悲剧

脚在鞋里，有着难熬的寂寞
它是矿工，钻在黑暗的煤层
幻想着星空，甚至幻想着喧嚣的街市
即便有狮的喉咙，也像烧断线的喇叭
只散出焦烂的气味

因为鞋，脚一生爱上了抱怨
不知道，它刚躲过马路上的危险
不知道，鞋正替它经历户外的严冬
不知道，鞋正帮它找出未来的长路

脚的怨气无穷无尽——
我把身体交给了你，却没有换来自由
我像骨架一样撑着你，却得不到半点感恩
我关在笼中，只得到你赐予的脚气

鞋说：是啊，是我穿过了风暴
才没有走漏你偷情的秘密
是我磨掉一层层硬皮，才让你白嫩得像新娘

睡觉前，脚气得甩脱鞋：
“你看，没有了我，你连苦难都没有了引擎！”

## Shoes and Feet

Shoes want to look up at the world
Including the enemy that's so tall and big
But it can't look up at the shadow crouched on the ground
Including the unfocused eyes in the dark
So they step over the long tragedy of shadow

Inside shoes, feet suffer a terrible loneliness
They're coal miners
Imagining the sky and noisy street market
Through a lion's throat, burning like a broken
Speaker, emitting the stink of scorch

Because of shoes, feet fall in love with complaining
They have no idea they have just escaped the accident
    on the highway
No idea how shoes endure long winters
How they seek the long journey into future

Feet complain endlessly:
I gave you everything, yet I still have no freedom
I hold you up with my skeleton, yet you never say thank you
I live in your cage. All I got in return is athlete foot

Shoes reply: yes, I walk through storms
So you can keep your secret of many affairs
I shed layers of skin, so you can look tender and white
    like a bride

Before sleep, feet take off their shoes in anger:
Look, without me, you won't even have an engine for
    your suffering

## 绳子

它曾经是蛇，在我心里爬动
我不习惯，它蛰伏在奶奶床下
它还会晒太阳，用脊梁、衣服、被子
在院子里架一座拉索桥

有时，它是缠住小偷的蟒蛇
众人对小偷的殴打，令我怀疑绳子的立场
搬家时，它是忠实的牧羊犬
把慌里慌张的物品，赶回车厢

它帮我系牢鞋子，坚持了五十年
飞尘中它屏住的咳嗽，比我写的字还多
有时，它也像绿萝的藤叶垂下
充满垂泪的忧伤——
它不想闲着，老和空虚约会

现在，它成了策展人
躲在画背后，满墙举着画
我知道，它是画背后的一根弦
只有心静，才听得见它为画配的乐

## Rope

It used to be a snake, slithering in my heart
I feared it as it crouched under grandma's bed
It loved the sun, using its spine, clothes and blankets
To build a cable bridge in the yard

Sometimes it became a python strangling a thief
As the crowd beat up the wretched man, I began to doubt
what it stood for
When we moved, it worked like a loyal sheep dog
Shepherding the hapless furniture into the truck

It helped tie my shoelace, 50 years long
In the dust. It forced back more coughs than the words I
wrote
Sometimes, it draped like a vine
Its leaves full of tearful sorrow
It hated being idle and hated meeting up with the void

Later it became a curator
Hiding in the back, holding up art on the wall
I know the rope is now a string behind each painting
You can hear their harmony, if you quiet your heart

## 奶奶的花折扇

夏夜，它是我手上的风帆
让我在大人的小道消息中航行
它也是蚊子眼中的台风
让蚊子结束对我的毒吻

在太阳已经熄火的炉门前
它试着递给我月亮的全部凉意
哪怕星光的歌唱是无声的
它照样朝我扇出，星星的一口口叹气

那时，穷据说是历史的安排
我用力扇出人人信任的春风
仿佛我的另一只手臂，是翅膀
云在飞，月在飞，星在飞
只有我扇动的手臂，让我停在露天的竹床

花折扇的开屏，常让我眩晕
我仿佛窥见，里面住着一只孔雀
情愿让它朝我，刮上好多年的孤独之风

## Grandma's Flower Fan

Summer night, it was a sail in my hands
Sailing through the wind of adult gossip and news
For mosquitoes, it was a hurricane
Blowing away stinging kisses from my tender skin

In front of the furnace of the setting sun
It tried to hand me the coolness of the moon
Even if the stars sang without a sound
It still fanned their sighing into my ears

Poor data and lies were part of history, I was told
I fanned and fanned, making spring wind that everyone
  could trust
My other arm became a wing
Everything was flying: clouds, moon, stars
But my fanning arm stayed behind on the bamboo bed
  under the sky

Grandma's flower fan opened and shut, giving me vertigo
I thought I had a glimpse of a peacock in her folding hand
I wish it had blown many years of solitude at me

## 静夜思

傍晚的广场舞，是镰刀
在收割母亲的晚年

他不知家谱或月亮
谁会是深夜的向导

家谱用沉默，掩饰它还活着
蒙尘的蛛网，是它悄悄发出的芽

家谱里的名字，守着富贵的八字
个个装作没有受伤

他坐在灯下，知道祖先们的命运
在窗外的星空，悄悄绽放

灯下的影子，从不声明
它不是黑人，只是日子的发票

他盼着用心跳，兑换寺庙的撞钟声

## Silent Night

Dancing at dusk on the public square feels like a sickle
That harvests mother's twilight years

He doesn't know his family tree or moon
Who will guide him through the deep night

The family tree hides its life in silence
The spiderweb has sprouted through dust

Each name on the family tree guards a fortune
Each pretends nobody ever got hurt

Sitting under the lamp, he watches his ancestors' fate
Open quietly in the night sky outside his window

The shadow under the light never utters a word:
It is not black, just a receipt from daily life

He hopes to trade the sounds of temple bells for
his heartbeats

## 姑姑的照片

姑姑扮青衣的照片，是我书房的装饰
她每天用戏装之美，给我的人生打气
那时，她的命运正在汉剧中高飞
家史还没有成为，一件刺向她的凶器

自从她被赶出剧团
悠长的唱腔是长巷，总把她引向戏台
直到砌墙的泥刀，在她手下铮铮响成曲调
直到一代名旦，变成炊烟中的巧妇

每个来书房的人，都赞叹她的美
这样的美，能给中年人补钙
能让修行人，心里开一朵莲花
能给我书房的寂静，安上灯塔

一股秋风想用吟唱，引出她的唱腔
我试着用伤感的诗句，为她配词
仿佛催促她重登戏台，但生锈的唱腔
已经适应安静
习惯让秋风做它的替身

## My Aunt's Photo

A photo of my aunt as a young woman hangs in my studio
Her beauty in her opera attire cheers up my life
At that time, her fortune rose high in the sky of Han Opera
Her family history was not yet a dagger in her heart

Since she was tossed out of the opera house
The long lane sings like an aria, taking her back to the stage
And the tools to make walls become melodies in her hands
Till a famous diva turns into a good wife in the kitchen

Every visitor admires her beauty
Her face, like calcium, fortifies the bones of
  a middle-aged man
It opens a lotus blossom in the hermit's heart
And turns on the lighthouse in the silent studio

A gust of autumn wind tries to bring out her song
I try to match her melody with melancholy poetry
As if it could push her back onto the stage, but her
  rusty voice
Has settled into peace
Into the autumn wind as her replacement

## 老花之眼

书放得再近，字也看不清了
那些被黑夜染黑的字，仿佛提醒我
要离书中的苦难远一点，远一点才能看清
字的额头上，那些刚愈合的黑疤

我戴上老花镜，每个字都飘着乌亮的黑发
它们拔掉的岁月白发，早已填满纸上的空白
也许字的每副黑棺里，都躺着好几条人命
我从小就用的字，里面的悲剧我数得清吗？

老花的眼，还会闪光
会把罚款五千，看成罚款五十万
那是暗示，老花的活着已不怕讹诈、惊吓？
当我把111路，看成111111路
那是暗示，111111路曾在火星开通过？
当闪光，让所有的字都长出彗星的尾巴
那是暗示，我们的文明随时也会返祖吗？

五年了，看不清倒让我想得更清
看不清别人的皱纹，倒把别人都看成健身高人
每天在高人中跋涉，连念头也像高人的长跑
每天都留下一个奔向远方的公里数

## Presbyopia

No matter how close I bring books to my face, I still can't
  read the words
Dyed black by the inky night, as if reminding me:
Get away from the pain in the book, if you want to see it
  more clearly
On the forehead of each word, black scars are healing

I put on glasses, now black hair floats across each word
It pulls white hair from life to fill the empty space on page
Maybe a word is a black coffin. Each holds a few lives
Can I count every tragedy in every word I've used?

My blurry eyes also flash light
They turn a 5000 yuan fine into 500,000
As if suggesting in my blurry age I no longer need to
  fear extortion?
When I see Highway 111 as Highway 111111
Is it hinting that this 1111111 highway would take me
  to Mars?
When the flashing light gives each word a comet tail
Is it saying our civilization is regressing to a stone age?

It's been five years. I think more clearly with my blurry sight
I can't see wrinkles, so everyone becomes an athlete
Trudging among them, my thoughts start running marathons
Recording how many miles are left till the future

## 两盆绿萝

题记：我买来两盆绿萝，让藤叶从楼顶垂下

一盆下方，是能攀援的墙壁
一年过去，它已让藤叶够到地板
它经历了锻炼体魄的长跑
让害羞的少年，长成了勇敢的青年
哪怕需要跳崖，也不怕摔到地上
它向有缺点的我，伸着劝诫的舌头？
哪怕话不投机，也不离不弃？
它心怀愧疚，让道歉的头向大地越垂越低？

另一盆下方，是让书沉睡的书架
绿萝却一直不让藤叶出发
我盯着它，看不出它有更多的睡意
它怀疑，我让它垂下的善意？
它担心，从楼顶落下，就像垃圾被人抛下？
莫非它爱书，要留在书架的上方
像眉毛呵护眼睛那样，呵护书的美梦？
它要永远登高，看清书能看清的远方？

一盆，对地板上的生活，伸手想抓住？
另一盆，守着书架，过着内心生活？
也许它们，代表我的两种愿望
每一种，都有每一种的棱角

## Devil's Ivy

I bought two pots of Devil's Ivy, its leaves dangling from
  the ceiling

Below one plant is the wall for climbing
After a year, the leaves have reached the floor
Like training for long distance running
A shy teenager has grown into a brave young man
Not afraid of falling to the ground, even jumping off a cliff
Is it sticking out its tongue at my failures?
Will it not abandon me, even if we can't communicate?
Is it bending its head to the earth, lower and lower,
  with guilt?

Under the other plant are the shelves where books sleep
The Devil's Ivy never lets its leaves depart
I stare at it, can't tell if it's been sleeping
Is it doubting my intention to let it hang?
Is it worried to fall from the ceiling like trash?
Maybe it hangs on the shelf because it loves books
Guarding their dreams like brows guarding eyes
Or it wants to climb up, to see future, like books

One pot wants to grasp life on the floor
The other just wants to stay on the shelf, for an inner life
Maybe they both represent my wishes
Each with its own edges and corners

## 书包

书包是书最漂亮的衣服
也是故事最想住的房子
小时我斜挎着它，为自己的童年壮胆
它让铅笔和课本，在黑暗的密室幽会

我常忘了关上它的门
课本会上路，尝试像文字那样去远方
铅笔会逃走，想追上它表白过的落日
橡皮擦落到地上，发现擦不掉地上的阴影

有时，书包也用铅笔盒的哐当声
向我倾诉，作业本的纸是茫茫沙漠
每杆笔都是铁锹，用来种下字的树苗

多年后，我背上了双肩包
包里的东西与书包大同小异
签字笔睡觉的样子，与铅笔无异
书慢慢变老的肤色，也与课本相同

在纸的沙漠上，种下字的树苗
仍是笔的基本功
小时想跟文字去的远方，已在身边
当我走在大街上，仍会寻找
从前书包的那张顽皮的脸

## Bookbag

A bookbag makes the most beautiful clothes for books
A house that stories aspire to sleep in
I carried it across my shoulders to cheer up my childhood
It arranged rendezvous for pencils and notebooks

I often forgot to close its door
The notebooks took off, adventuring to distance places
  like words
Pencils escaped, catching up with the sunset they had drawn
The eraser fell on the floor, discovering a shadow it
  couldn't erase

Sometimes, the bookbag tells me stories
Through the clanking pencil box.
The homework paper is a desert
Each pencil is a shovel, planting trees of language

Many years later, I carried a backpack
Things inside looked the same as my bookbag
The sleeping pen I used for signature looks the same as
  the pencil
My books and notebooks yellow with age

In the paper desert, the word saplings
Laid the foundation for my pen
The faraway place my childhood dreamed of has arrived
When I walk on the street, I still seek
The smiling face of my old bookbag

## 煤油灯

我早已失去煤油灯
那是童年夜里，在作业边升起的太阳——
奶奶安上灯罩的刹那，灯芯像要发完一生的光

奶奶是管辖灯光的女王
准许爷爷捧起杜诗，反复温习古代的落魄

数学本里的优，让我一夜都翘着尾巴
爷爷说，我教你《诗经》吧
我不答应，他不知《诗经》在学校
已变得污秽，不知我眼中的煤油灯罩
还把污点，纷纷投在他的脸上

奶奶趁着煤油灯的夕照，赶制冬天的棉衣
一副用旧的老花镜，让她攒下劳动的学问

那时我不知，灯光照着我，就像照着一片废墟
照着爷爷恨铁不成钢的痛心
到如今，我的心里仍能摸到那盏煤油灯——

当我捧起《诗经》，是故去的爷爷在教我
当我戴上老花镜，是故去的奶奶在教我
御寒之术

## Kerosene Lamp

I lost my kerosene lamp long ago
The sun rose to shine on my homework when I was a child
The wick burnt its entire life after Grandma screwed on
the cover

Grandma was the queen in charge of light
She let Grandpa pick up books, retrieving the lost souls
in Du Fu's poetry

All night long I walked like a peacock for the A I got in math
Let me teach you The Book of Poetry, said Grandpa
I refused. He didn't know that poetry had turned into
Dirt at school, didn't know that the kerosene lamp
Was throwing stains on his face

Grandma was sewing winter clothes, in the sunset of
the lamp
Earning the knowledge through work with her
reading glasses

I didn't know then that the lamp shone its light on me, as if
on the ruins
It shone on Grandpa's disappointment: the iron that can't be
smelted into steel
I can still touch that kerosene lamp in my heart

Now when I hold The Book of Poetry, I know my deceased
Grandpa is teaching me
When I put on my reading glasses, it's my deceased
Grandma showing me
How to fight cold

## 北京的秋风

南京的秋风，只是
一股股发霉的口气
被吹到的人，知道风里没有仇恨

当我来到北京，才听到了风的哭泣
风还把我当作冷战的敌人
把我张口的问候，一劈两半
它还用整夜的厉声，训斥我
阻拦谎话从梦里上路

太阳升起时，我继续听着风声
猜测风里藏着多少炸药？
街边的那些树，因被风雇佣了
努力显出收割落叶的丰收模样

我知道，因为风大
我身上有再多的酒气，仍嫌不够
有再多裹紧命运的衣裳，仍嫌单薄

北京的风啊，我多想知道
你何时才有倦意？
对人们加班中的命运，你已有新的安排？

我只是来自南方的一个诗人
那里的秋风再大，也啼不出血
它顶多朝水面，吐上一层抱怨的口沫
表示，冬天正在登陆

## The Fall Wind in Beijing

The fall wind in Nanjing is nothing but
Moldy breath. Those who feel its blow
Know the wind carries no hatred

Only in Beijing, I heard the wind sobbing
It treats me like a cold-war foe
Slicing my greeting in half
Scolding me with its shrill voice all night long
Blocking lies to escape my dreams

When the sun came out, I kept listening to the wind
Guessing how many tons of explosives were hidden in
  its gusts
Trees along sidewalks, sold to the wind
Tried to show the appearance of a great harvest

I know, because of the howling wind
No matter how much I drink, it's not enough to keep up
  my spirits
No matter how tightly I wrap my coat around my destiny,
  it's still too thin

Oh, wind from Beijing, how I want to know
When you'll get tired!
And what's your new plan for those destined to work over-
time?

I'm just a poet from the South
No matter how big, the wind from that soil can't draw blood
The worst it can do is to spit some foamy complaints
  to water's surface
To show that winter is about to land

## 战争

我独立山巅
心里没有战争

战争，却在远方
试穿着几个国家的衣袍

口号是风
早已吹彻地球的城乡
但，再也惊扰不了死者

## War

I stand on top of a mountain
No war in my heart

But far away
It's trying on a few countries' cloaks

Wind blows the trumpet of slogans
Blasting across cities and countryside
Yet, it cannot longer disturb the dead

## 镜子

你无法藏身，镜子让你醒在残酷的皱纹里
你的泪珠，被镜子读成闪亮的星辰
你想找回的青春，被镜子读成与你重逢

你的小狗，对着镜子狂吠
认定镜子里的小狗不懂事
面对它的愤怒，居然一声不吭

你和小狗，都对镜子不满
都想对着镜子干点什么
你涂脂抹粉，被镜子读成脸上积满灰尘
小狗的狂吠，被镜子听成摇滚

## Mirror

No place to hide, the mirror jolts you into cruel wrinkles
It reads your tears as shining stars
And thinks your effort to look young is your fear for
  the reunion

In the face of the puppy's angry bark
The mirror says nothing

Neither you or the dog are pleased with the mirror
Both are determined to make it pay
You put on makeup, but the mirror thinks your face
  is covered in dust
And the dog's barking, well it's just some rock'n roll

## 手相

三十岁，我才认识手掌
认定一根叉子似的掌纹，代表你会离婚
如果一根掌纹，不断把命运推离掌丘
它是说，你今后要抑郁了
中指上，还藏着你挫折的刻痕

唉，我当了数年的半仙
介入了他人的生活
我说你会生病，你剩下的日子便成了药片
我说你会出国，你就把母语当成生活的累赘
我说你会出家，工作就成了对你的惩罚

我解读掌纹时，有太多的人发出尖叫
那是幸福被践踏时的惨痛
人为什么非要用未来，毁掉现在？
停在此刻该多好，可以用阳光的毛巾
擦净脸上的阴沉

满手掌纹，可以是满手锁链、满手诀别
也可以是满手笑纹、满手出路
如果你乐意享受现在这把摇椅
如果你非要搭上现在这趟班车，去墓地

## Palm Reading

I learned how to read palms at 30
A fork line means you'll be divorced
A line that pushes your fate away from the base
Means you'll be doomed to depression
And the middle finger hides the traumas in your life

Oy, I've been such a demi-deity for years
Slipping into people's privacy
I predict you'll fall ill, your remaining days filled with pills
I say you'll go abroad where your mother tongue becomes
  a burden
I say you'll become a monk, and your job will feel like
  a punishment

My palm readings have made too many people scream
From the pain as their happiness is trashed
Why do we destroy our present with the future?
Why not pause now and here, wiping the shadows
Off our face with a towel soaked in sunshine?

The lines on my palm could be chains and goodbyes
They could be laughing lines, lacing my hand with
  infinite paths
All depends upon if you want to enjoy the rocking chair
  of NOW
Or insist on getting on the bus driving towards a graveyard

## 收音机

最初，只有一台矿石收音机
我惊诧它会送来百里外的声音
我和表哥拉上门，徒劳地想偷听敌台
风那么大，我们断言，是风折断了声音的翅膀

等到新的收音机，让声音飞过了海峡
我们又相信，有些声音已在半途迷路
一不小心，收音机又送来一个美国
我们半夜竖着耳朵，靠声音里的养分过活

今天，这台收音机的声音不再翻山越岭
它在抽屉，已冬眠了三十年
几个收听它的人，早已走出青春的迷途
如今，他们像抽屉里的收音机一样沉默，这就足够了
他们登一登钟山，这就足够了

## Radio

At first, it was a crystal radio
I was shocked by the voice from hundreds of miles away
Cousin and I closed the door, trying to hear the
  enemy's station
But it was too windy, so the voice's wings must be broken,
  we concluded

Then came the new radio that could bring the voice across
  the sea
We believed some of the voices must be falling from the sky
Then out of nowhere, the radio brought us America
We listened to its voice at midnight, living on its nutrients.

Now the radio no longer climbs over the mountains
For 20 years, it's been hibernating in the drawer
Those who listened to its voice are out of the maze of youth
They are silent like the radio
Feeling content to walk up Mount Bell once in a while

## 舞会

我跳过的那些舞，曾打开了我的生活
那些旋转的华尔兹，如今只有落叶用它打转

一对被舞步锁住的人，他俩的孤独变轻还是变重了？
跳着约定俗成的舞步，憧憬也约定俗成吗？

我经历过跳舞的青春
曾用黑灯舞把青春，跳成家人的责备
跳成噎住老师的长叹
那些已经绝迹的舞步，它们还在赶往今天的途中？

我那时不知，自己是在孤独的深处
舞步旋出的，是青春的迷宫
但我忘不掉一起跳舞的人
为了憧憬，他们宁可重复舞步

很多时刻——舞步像舌头
会发出无人能懂的声音
它们像月光，会用梦照亮舞者的一生

## Dance Party

I used to dance to open my life
The music that whirled waltz now swirls up fallen leaves

The pair is synced. Does that make their loneliness
Lighter? Their dance follows a routine.
Does that make their future routine?

I too went through a dancing youth
My black-light dance sidestepped parental scolding
And choked my teacher's sighs
Those dance steps, are they still trying to catch up today?

I had no idea I was deep in solitude
My dance created a maze of loneliness
But I remember my partners, willing
To repeat every step towards happiness

Sometimes the dance flickers like a tongue
Making freakish sounds nobody can decode
And it'd take one's whole life to escape its maze

## 夏夜银河

小时，我睡在露天的竹床
一睁眼，就能看见天上的晶亮冰雕
我需要它的冷，和它的一宿不动的睡眠
姑姑唱情歌落的泪，已被它冻成满天冰晶

我愿意用一生，守着深夜的那一刻——
奶奶在梦中，访问了她的前世
爷爷用鼾声，参加了汉朝的战争
只有我被蚊子及时叫醒，目睹天上刚冻住的一场风暴

我试着从风暴中，找出一个女同学的脸
班上数她最沉默，天上有她的一对酒窝
却空空如也，我只能借蚊子的嗡嗡情话
让自己微醉，找回替她抄作业的心跳

黑夜用黑漆的犁，翻开天上最富饶的土地
我的未来是种子，已撒入刀口一样的沟壑
我聆听着它的沉默，和闪烁其词
它向我展示，天上有那么多舌头，我听到的却是无声

小时的银河，就是我的学校
它常摆出科学课上的动物标本
向我展示黑烟与白烟有何不同
它像路灯，让我成为不怕走夜路的男孩

## The Milky Way in Summer Nights

When I was a child, I slept on a bamboo bed in the open
I could see the icy sculpture in the sky when I opened
    my eyes
I needed its coolness, its motionless sleep through the night
And my aunt sang songs, her tear frozen like crystals
    in the sky

I'm willing to guard that midnight moment with my life
How Grandma revisited past lives in her dreams
How Grandpa joined a war from the Han Dynasty through
    his snores
How mosquitoes woke me up on time to witness the
    frozen storm

I tried to find my classmate's face in the storm
She was the quietest in class. I thought I saw her dimples
But no, only mosquitoes buzzing. Their love songs
Intoxicated me, my heart beating wildly as if I were doing
    her homework again

With a black plough, night cuts open the sky's rich field
My future is a seed, sowed into the ditch sharper than a knife
I listen to its silence, how it minces words, displaying
Endless tongues in heaven. Yet all I hear is its soundlessness

The Milky Way was my childhood school
It put out a full display of specimens from science books
Showing me the difference between black and white smoke
Training a little boy, like patient streetlights, to walk
    in the dark without fear

现在，城市的夜空满是黑发
这些扮相年轻的黑发，不会是假发？
那些智慧的银发，都掉落进了贫穷年代？

今夜，天照样黑下去，银河却未升起来
不再像我小时，会慷慨摆出它的所有银器

Now, the city's night sky is covered with black hair
It appears young, how real is it?
And where's wisdom's silver hair, fallen into an
impoverished age?

Tonight, the sky is darkening as usual, but the Milky Way
no longer rises
To offer its silverware with generosity, the way it used to,
when I was a child

## 锁

它只烦恼活着的人
该把什么锁进来？该把什么放出去？
它锁进婚姻、金钱、激情和房产证
放出事业、偷情、儿女和山河

锁主张一妻多夫
把它女性的身躯，同时交给几把男性的钥匙
锁也重色轻友，六亲不认
不摸着钥匙的胴体，它不给主人开门

锁也是秘密的孪生兄弟
它哪怕有口，钥匙哪怕有舌头
它俩也不说话
它俩只用沉默美化历史

锁也像伤兵，想用裂开的伤口，吞咽光明
钥匙像一只扑灯的蛾子
冲进去，却只找到梦的黑影

## Lock

It only bothers the living
Whom to lock in, whom to lock out
It locks up marriage, money, passion, property
It lets loose career, cheating, children, rivers and mountains

Lock supports polyandry
It allows a woman's body to be set for a few male keys
It likes sex better than friendship and cares nothing
    about family
It won't open the door to the master unless he has the key

Lock is the twin brother of secrets
Even if it has a mouth, its key has a tongue
It remains silent
To glorify the heart's secret

Lock is a soldier, swallowing light with its open wound
Key, on the other hand, is a moth to the flames
It flops inside, only to find the broken shadows of night

## Biographies

Huang Fan (黄梵, 1963–) is a leading writer of poetry and fiction, known for his unflinching confrontation of contemporary issues in China with dry humor and dark lyricism. His books in Chinese include *Insomniac Moon*, *Elegies of Nanjing*, *The Eleventh Commandment*, *The Floating Colors*, *Until Youth Disappears*, *Girls School Teacher*, *Wandering China*, *Empire of Imagery*, *Strumming a Rope*, *The Human Museum*, and *Dyslexia*. "Middle Age" was included in *One Hundred Poems for One Hundred Years of Chinese Modern Poetry*, and the editor of *United Daily News* called him the mainland poet of most interest to the Taiwanese reader. When his novel *The Eleventh Commandment* was serialized in Sina.com.cn's literary section, it received over 3 million hits and was rated one of two "must-read" novels for young people to read. He has won numerous prizes, including the Boao International Poetry Prize, the China Good Poetry Prize, the Beijing Literary Prize, the Jinling Literary Prize, the Zhongshan Literary Prize, the West Literary Prize, the Fangcao Biennial Top Ten Prize for Poetry, the Zijin Mountain Literature Prize, and the Writer's Golden Prize for Short Story, World Chinese Weekly Literature Award, and Yanhe Most Popular among Readers Award. Appearances include Florence International Poetry Festival, the Qinghai Lake Poetry Festival, Toronto International Festival of Authors, Macau Literary Festival, Havana International Festival of Poetry, and Singapore World Book Day Literature under an April Sky. Translations of his poetry in English has been featured in *Granta*, *Poetry*, *Push Open the Window* (Copper Canyon 2011), and *A Public Space* and has been praised by English-language language poets aesthetically diverse as Robert Hass, Forrest Gander, Ron Padgett, J.H. Prynne and Phillip Lopate. Besides English, his works have been translated into Italian, German, Greek, French, Japanese, Farsi, Spanish and Korean.

黄梵（1963 -）是杰出诗人和小说家，以其冷幽默和黑色抒情的方式直面中国当代问题而闻名。他的著作有《月亮已失眠》《南京哀歌》《第十一诫》《浮色》《等待青春消失》《女校先生》《中国走徒》《意象的帝国》《用绳子弹奏》《人性的博物馆》《阅读障碍》等。《中年》入选《中国新诗百年百首》《联合报》主编称他是台湾最有读者缘的大陆诗人。他的长篇小说《第十一诫》在新浪读书原创连载时点击率超过300万被网络推重为新时期最值得青年关注的两部小说之一。曾获博鳌国际诗歌奖、中国好诗奖、北京文学奖、金陵文学奖、中山文学奖、西部文学奖、芳草双年十佳诗歌奖、紫金山文学奖、短篇小说作家金奖、世界华文周刊文学奖、延河最受读者欢迎奖等。受邀参加佛罗伦萨国际诗歌节、青海湖诗歌节、多伦多国际作家节、澳门文学节、哈瓦那国际诗歌节、新加坡“世界读书日文学四月天”。他的诗歌英译已发表在《格兰塔》《诗刊》《推开一扇窗》（铜峡谷2011）和《公共空间》等，并得到罗伯特·哈斯、福雷斯特·甘德、罗恩·帕吉特、J.H.蒲龄恩和菲利普·洛佩特等英语诗人的赞誉。除英语外，他的作品还译成意大利语、德语、希腊语、法语、日语、波斯语、西班牙语和韩语等。

Margaret Ross is the author of two books of poetry, *A Timeshare* (Omnidawn, 2015) and *Saturday* (The Song Cave, 2024). Her poems and translations have appeared in *Granta*, *Harper's*, *The Paris Review* and *POETRY*. Her work has been supported by a Harper-Schmidt Fellowship, a Wallace Stegner Fellowship, a MacDowell Fellowship, a Fulbright grant and a VSC/Luce Foundation Chinese Poetry & Translation Fellowship. She currently lives in Saskatchewan.

玛格丽特-罗斯著有两本诗集《A Timeshare》（Omnidawn，2015 年）和《Saturday》（The Song Cave，2024 年）。她的诗作和译文曾发表在《格兰塔》《哈泼斯杂志》《巴黎评论》和《诗刊》上。她的作品曾获得富布赖特奖学金、VSC/亨利.卢斯基金会中国诗歌与翻译奖学金，以及芝加哥大学，斯坦福大学 和麦克道威尔文艺营的奖学金。她目前居住在萨斯喀彻温省。

Josh Stenberg（石峻山）is an Associate Professor in Chinese Studies at the University of Sydney. He is the author of *Minority Stages: Sino-Indonesian Performance and Public Display* (University of Hawai'i Press, 2019), the translator or editor of six books of contemporary Chinese fiction and poetry and an author of poetry and fiction. The holder of an Australian Research Council Discovery Early Career Research Award, his recent articles have been published in leading journals of theatre and literature. Recent research outputs includes Research on *Southern Drama Research Abroad* (Zhonghua shuju). Works appearing in 2022 include *Kunqu Masters on Chinese Theatrical Performance* (as editor; Anthem) and *Liyuanxi: Chinese Pear Garden Theatre* (Bloomsbury) and his work as editor on a special issue on Nanjing Arts and Literature on *Perspectives on Arts and Humanities Asia*. In 2023 he published translations of Su Tong's short fiction *Missives from the Masses* (ACA Publishing) and his work as co-editor of *Asian Ethnicity* on Chinese communities of Philippines and Indonesia. He has held Fulbright, Canada Social Sciences and Humanities Research Council, Australian Academy of the Humanities and Indonesian Ministry of Education and Culture grants and held leadership positions in the Chinese Studies Association of Australia and the Australian Society for Asian Humanities.

石峻山，悉尼大学中国研究副教授。出版有《少数民族舞台：中-印度尼西亚表演与公开展示》(夏威夷大学出版社，2019年)，翻译和编辑出版六本中国当代小说和诗歌，着有诗歌、小说、研究文章等，在戏剧和文学核心杂志发表，获澳大利亚研究委员会发现早期职业研究奖。近期研究著作包括《南戏域外传播研究》（合着，2021，中华书局），2022年主编的《昆曲大师谈中国戏剧表演》等，2023年出版苏童中短篇小说集《集群众来信》(ACA出版)等。获得富布赖特基金会、加拿大社会科学与人文研究理事会、澳大利亚人文学院和印度尼西亚教育与文化部等资助，在澳大利亚中国研究协会和澳大利亚亚洲人文学会担任领导职务。

Wang Ping published 15 books of poetry & prose, including *The River within*（MadHat 2023），*My Name Is Immigrant* (Hanging Loose 2021), *Life of Miracles along Yangtze and Mississippi* (Georgia U, 2018), *Aching for Beauty* (Anchorage 2001)，*The Last Communist Virgin* (Coffee House 2016), *New Generation: Poetry from China Today* (Hanging Loose 2000), and others . She's recipient of NEA, Bush, Lannan, McKnight Fellowships, AWP Book Award, and many others. She's also a dancer, photographer, installation artist, competitive rower. *New York Times* featured her poetry and rowing for "the Story of the Day" in 2013. She's founder/director of Kinship of Rivers project, Poetry Professor Emerita, Macalester College.

北大英语系文学学士，AAAOM 中医硕士，纽约大学比较文学博士, 美国麦克乐思特大学终身教授，主教诗歌创作，出版了15本英文诗歌、小说、翻译，多次受邀国际诗歌节、美国电台电视演讲，包括BBC, CBS, NPR，MPR, PBS, 纽约林肯中心，纽约时报，耶鲁，普林斯顿等；获多项文学大奖，包括美国诗歌基金奖，布什诗歌奖，蓝能文学奖，麦克奈特文学奖，明州图书奖，亚洲研究图书奖，美国杰出移民奖，委内瑞拉"国际优秀诗人奖"，"明州先锋诗歌桂冠诗人"。中文作品发表于《北京周报》，《作家》，《草原》，《诗歌月刊》，刊》，《美文》，《青岛文学》等。她也热爱舞蹈、摄影、装置艺术、划艇等体育和艺术 。《纽约时报》在2013年将她的诗歌和赛艇运动选为"每日故事"进行专题报道。

GP
Gugin Press
New York / Shanghai